BUDDHISM IN THE MODERN WORLD

BUDDHISM
IN THE
MODERN WORLD

K. J. SAUNDERS

GYAN

Published by

GYAN

Gyan Publishing House
5, Ansari Road
Daryaganj, New Delhi-110002
Phone: 011-47034999, 9811692060
E-mail: books@gyanbooks.com

Distribution Network
gyanbooks.com
India, USA, Canada, UK, Australia

ISBN: 978-93-6780-208-3 (HB)

First Published, 1922

2nd Impression 2024

Printed at: Gyan Press, Delhi.

BUDDHISM IN THE MODERN WORLD
Author: K. J. SAUNDERS

BUDDHISM IN THE MODERN WORLD

BY

K. J. SAUNDERS

AUTHOR OF

"THE STORY OF BUDDHISM," "GOTAMA BUDDHA," ETC.

PROFESSOR OF THE HISTORY OF RELIGION, BERKELEY
AND LECTURER IN THE UNIVERSITY OF CALIFORNIA

LONDON

SOCIETY FOR PROMOTING
CHRISTIAN KNOWLEDGE

NEW YORK AND TORONTO: THE MACMILLAN COMPANY

1922

PREFACE

THERE are many books on Buddhism, and to produce a new one almost demands an apology. Yet most of them deal with the dead past, and Buddhism is a living religion which is showing remarkable powers of revival and adaptation. This is a movement of so great significance that I hope this small volume may prove of value, not only to missionaries but to all sympathetic students of a religion which has played an immense part in the world's history, and which is still a dominant influence in the lives of scores of millions. During twelve years of somewhat intimate study of Buddhist countries I have found that while there is much that is degenerate there is much that is very noble, and the object of this little book is to estimate the living forces of the religion rather than to emphasise its weaknesses. It is at once more scientific and more worth while to look at the strong than at the weak points of a religion, and there is an increasing school of missionary thought which believes in building the Christian Church of Asia upon the great foundations laid through so many centuries. Not only is it true that God has not left Himself without a witness amongst these peoples; it is even truer that during the long and on the whole noble history of the expansion of Buddhism His Spirit has been at work. I am convinced that any who really study this remarkable chapter in human history will come to this conclusion, if they have any belief whatsoever in a meaning in history and in a Divine Providence.

The missionary amongst Buddhist peoples should aim at studying all that is noble and of good repute, whilst of course he will not shut his eyes to what is degenerate and unworthy, and inasmuch as an increasing number of missionary teachers are doing me the honour to consult me as to the method of approach to their Buddhist friends, I venture to dedicate this small volume to them as a token of hearty sympathy in the noble work that they are doing in seeking to fulfil the age-long purposes of God. I think that many of them agree with me that already a nobler form of Christianity is being produced on Asiatic soil than that which we have brought thither, and it may well be in the providence of God that a new and splendid era of Church History is opening up as these responsive and religious peoples of the Orient are captured by the Gospel of Christ. In spite of the failures of Christendom and of our divided Christianity the whole of Asia reverences the historic Jesus, and from her contact with His Spirit is at once reforming and revivifying her ancient faiths. This process is of immense significance and her best spirits, even when they do not call themselves Christian, are frank to confess how much they owe to Him and how much there is in their old faiths which will need to die in order that they may live again, purified and deepened. That Asia is increasingly becoming

Christian in its standards of thought and conduct is evident to any unbiased observer, and one of the most remarkable proofs of the authenticity and originality of our faith is this—that it is at once reforming and fulfilling the ancient faiths of Asia. What it did with the religions of Rome and Greece it is already doing with the nobler religions of the Orient; and true missionaries of Christ are at work upon a task of incomparable dignity and significance,

These brief sketches are based upon ten years of intimate association with Buddhists in Southern and Eastern Asia.

Inasmuch as I have only been on the borders of Tibet I have not written here of Tibetan Buddhism. It is very degenerate and so mixed with Tantric Hinduism as to demand separate and different handling: it is very clear that missionary work is urgently needed to free the people of Tibet from a tyranny which is unworthy of the great name of the Buddha.

K. J. S.

BERKELEY,
January, 1922.

TABLE OF CONTENTS

II. BUDDHISM IN CEYLON

III. BUDDHISM IN SIAM

IV. CONTRASTED TYPES OF BUDDHIST RELIGIOUS LIFE IN SOUTHERN ASIA

V. BUDDHISM AS A LIVING WORLD RELIGION

VI. THE MISSIONARY APPROACH TO MODERN BUDDHISM IN SOUTHERN ASIA

II. BUDDHISM IN EASTERN ASIA

I. BUDDHISM IN JAPAN

II. BUDDHISM IN CHINA

BUDDHISM IN THE MODERN WORLD

I. BUDDHISM IN SOUTHERN ASIA

I. BUDDHISM IN BURMA

1. At the great Pagoda in Rangoon.

LET us visit the great *Shwe Dagon* pagoda in Rangoon, one of the living centres of the Buddhist world, where amidst a splendid grove of palms and forest trees the golden spire rises high above a vast platform crowded with shrines and images of the Buddha. Far below is the teeming city bathed in golden light, and humming with life; here all is still save for the rustle of leaves and the tinkling of innumerable bells upon the great pagoda pinnacle, and the shouting of a class of boys in the monastery school near by.

(a) *A Monastic School.*—Some two score of them are seated round a kindly old monk in his faded yellow robe. And all are shouting at the top of their voices repeating in unison certain words, of whose meaning they do not seem to think!

(b) *Its Moral Teaching.*—As we draw near we realise that these are phrases from a popular Buddhist book known as *Mingala Thot*, a summary of the Buddhist beatitudes, which describe the happy life of the Buddhist layman. First they shout a word of Pāli * and then a word of Burmese, and lastly the whole phrase. There are twelve verses, of which the following is typical :—

> " Tend parents, cherish wife and child,
> Pursue a blameless life and mild :
> Do good, shun ill and still beware
> Of the red wine's insidious snare ;
> Be humble, with thy lot content,
> Grateful and ever reverent."

Many times must these phrases be droned through before they are learned by heart, but gradually their meanings sink in and simple explanations and grammatical notes by the teacher help his class to understand as well as to learn. These moral maxims still exert a powerful influence for good.

(c) *Its Religious Instruction.*—Another favourite lesson is a short summary of the excellent qualities of the " Three Jewels " of Buddhism—the Buddha, his Order of Monks, and his Law or teaching ; and another celebrates eight victories of the Buddha over enemies temporal and spiritual. Having mastered these preliminary books, the boys will learn the chief *Jātakas,* a strange medley of folklore dressed up in Buddhist guise, and purporting to be stories of the various sacrificial existences of the founder of Buddhism, Sākyamuni, before he became a

* The ancient and still the classic language of S. Buddhism in which its scriptures are preserved. It is used religiously, much as Latin is used in the Roman Catholic services.

Buddha. Buddhism is not only a body of moral teachings, but a religion with an elaborate system of beliefs, which makes very great demands upon the faith of its worshippers, and some of these beliefs are embodied in these stories of the former lives of the Buddha. Others are conveyed in legends and hymns, in popular summaries and proverbial sayings universally known and used by the people.

(d) *The Importance of the Monks.*—This class of boys around the old monk represents an educational system which covers all Burma and has unbounded influence. It is an amazing fact that there are almost two monasteries to every village. While this constitutes an enormous drain upon the resources of the country, since all the monks retire from its active industrial life, and live upon the alms of the laity, it has, on the other hand, made Burma one of the most literate of all the lands of the East, with a larger percentage of men who can read and write than modern Italy. So great is the power of the monks that all boys, before they can be regarded as human beings, must undergo a form of ordination. It is not strange that some of them are caught by the lure of the monastic life and the glamour of the yellow robe: yet most of them, after a short experience, go back to the world.

The young *shin* or novice, who chooses to stay in a monastery, may in due course be admitted to ordination. At that time, dressed in princely robes, he celebrates the sacrifice of the founder of Buddhism, Sākyamuni, in leaving his royal state to become a mendicant. His head is shaved, his gorgeous clothes are taken away, and henceforward he is clad only in the yellow robe of the Buddhist monks, an order older, more widespread, and more picturesque than any other religious order in the world. He has "taken refuge in the Three Jewels," and now takes up the regular life of the monk. He goes out daily with a group of others to collect food for the monastery; he attends to the various needs of the older monks and carries on the simple household tasks assigned to him. A large portion of his time must be given to studies, until he has a good working knowledge of the three "Baskets," * *i.e.* the Discipline, the Narratives or Dialogues, and the Higher Religion, which make up the Buddhist canon. In course of time he may himself become a teacher.

Let us turn again to the shrine. The great sun is going down and the pagoda, splendid in the sunset as it changes from gold to purple and from purple to gray, and then to silver as the glorious moon rises, is thronged with devout worshippers. The monk prostrates himself before the jewelled alabaster image of Buddha. He seems unaware of the people around him, who honour him as a being of a superior order; or, if conscious of them, it is with a sense of his own aloofness. "Sabbā Dukkhā" (all is sorrow) he is murmuring: "Sabbā Anattā" (all is without abiding entity). Mechanically the lay-folk repeat with him the words which have been for twenty-five centuries the Buddhist challenge to the world, calling it away from the lure of the senses and the ties of family and home.

* The Tipitaka (Sanskrit, Tripitika) (1) *Vinaya;* (2) *Sutta;* (3) *Abhidhamma.* The Pāli scriptures were originally written on palm leaves and preserved, layer upon layer, in the three "baskets." This, at least, is one explanation of the use of this term.

Do the people really believe it? Let us look at this group of women before one of the many shrines on the spacious pagoda platform. Are they intent on giving up the world or on making the most of it? Are they persuaded that it is all sad and transient? Here kneels a young wife offering strands of her hair, and praying that her child may have hair as long and beautiful. Near by is an unhappy wife who prays that her husband may become as pure as the flower which she lays at the feet of the Buddha. Not far away is one very old and trembling woman who, after bowing to the impassive image and lighting her little candle before it, has turned back to pat a great old tree lest the *nat*, or spirit, which lives within, be offended. "The spirits are always malignant and have to be propitiated. The world-renowned one, is he not benign?" She must not risk offending this tree-spirit, in her desire to please the Buddha. "The Burman tries to keep both in mind and to serve them faithfully, for both may help to make this life pleasant; but he is most anxious concerning the demons. Whilst in every village in the country there is at least one pagoda and monastery, there is sure to be a spirit-shrine in every home, where the spirits are consulted and appeased before homes are built, marriages arranged, purchases made, or journeys undertaken." It is these things, after all, that make up life for most of us.

2. The Religious Values of Everyday Buddhism.

(a) *What Buddhism means for Burmese Women.*—It will be interesting to consider what Buddhism has to offer to such groups of women. Four sorts of appeal may be mentioned. In the first place Buddhism is a great social force, providing many festivals and giving much colour to everyday life. In theory it may be sad; in practice it is very cheerful. Even in Christian lands some women go to church to see the latest fashions; can we wonder that Burmese Buddhist women delight to gather on the platform of the beautiful pagoda for friendly intercourse and gossip? Again, they think of the order of monks as giving them the best chance to gain "merit." They recall that the Master taught that generous offerings to them are potent in bringing all kinds of benefits in this world, and even in helping the dead in the dim life of the underworld. The monks confer a favour by accepting alms; it is the donor who says "Thank you."

Another great source of enjoyment and instruction is the well-known Buddhist stories, told over and over again, often miraculous, always with a moral. They also reflect on the lives, which they know by heart, of certain great *Bodhisattvas*, or Buddhas in the making, "buds of the lotus," which later on burst into full bloom. One of the pictures in which they delight is that of Gotama * when he was a hare and jumped into the fire to feed a hungry Brahmin. Another picture more familiar and more poignant still, depicts his appearance as Prince Vessantara, giving away his wife and beloved children to a hunchback beggar. These stories exert an immense influence.

And finally, Buddhism influences Burmese women by appealing to their imagination and their love of

* Gotama is the Pāli form (common in S. Asia) of the Sanskrit Gautama, more familiar to Western readers.

mystery, with its solemn chanting, its myriad shrines, with their innumerable candles twinkling in the dusk, and the sexless sanctity of its monks. How wise and good they seem to be! Are they not custodians of the truth? Here one little woman is lifting a heavy stone weighing forty pounds; a monk has told her that if it seems heavy her prayer will surely be answered. To make assurance doubly sure, she may go and consult the soothsayer, whose little booth is near the shrine—a cheerful rogue, not without insight and a sense of humour—but she gives to the monk the supreme place, and pays him more generously!

A Burman acquaintance of mine, who was converted to Christianity, was asked by an old lady why he had deserted the "custom" of his people. "I am sick," he began, "of all this bowing down to the monks, and of all these offerings." "Stop, stop!" she cried, aghast. "You are destroying the whole religion of our nation!"

(b) *What it means for Burmese Men.*—Laymen in Burma are much like men elsewhere. Here is one who between prostrations before the image of Buddha keeps his long cheroot alive, and enjoys an occasional puff. He is like many men one meets, "making the best of both worlds." Yet to him too Buddhism makes a strong appeal, primarily because it is his heritage or, as he says, "the custom of Burma." The national feeling, which is alive in Burma as well as in all other parts of the East, resents Western influences, of which Christianity seems a part. Moreover, Buddhism strongly appeals to his habit of mind. He thinks he understands why there is inequality in human lot, why some are rich and some poor, some healthy and some diseased. He explains it as the working out of the law of *Kamma.** Men suffer now because they have sinned in a former birth. Listen to this conversation: Old U Hpay is telling a neighbour about a foolish old sister of his who has adopted a calf, and is petting it because its voice is so like that of her dead husband! While the old men chuckle at this quaint expression of her faith, yet they do believe that this is the law of life. Should you kill a mosquito it may be your mother-in-law in a new body, and still going strong! But Buddhism puts forth its greatest appeal at those times when there comes over its votaries a wistful yearning for something which this world has not given them. At these quiet moments, especially in the evening of life, when they are no longer concerned with making money or with the raising of a family, the appeal of *Nibbāna* † and its peace comes home to many. They do not feel sure of reaching it, nor do they fully understand what it means. Some of their monkish teachers tell them it will be annihilation, while others describe it as the extinction of all passion or a great calm. In either way *Nibbāna* † has its lure, especially to the world-weary. I have even known a Christian missionary who was tempted to long for the quiet and relief from the staleness and hurry of life which annihilation would bring. But he was weary and needed a holiday! Missionaries often do.

(c) *Buddhism and Children.*—Playing around, while the old people talk or pray, are always some

* Sanskrit, *Karma.*

† Sanskrit, *Nirvāna.*

children. Here a fat, naked baby takes a puff at his grandfather's cigar ; there a little girl, devoutly imitating what she sees her parents doing before the great image of Buddha, also lights her candle and offers her marigolds. The older children quickly begin to take their share in the religious life about them. In some of them is dawning a hero-worship of the great Buddha who has done so much for the world. This little girl thinks wistfully of her brother, so recently her playmate, but now a Buddhist novice, with shaven head and yellow robe, as remote from her and aloof as if he belonged to another world. Not much is taught to her and her girl-playmates : " they are only girls ! " But she is learning by what she sees, and she too is becoming a staunch Buddhist. There are some stalwart champions of Buddhism amongst the children, and the girls grow up, less instructed but not less devout than the boys.

(d) *The Attitude of Burmese Students.*—Every mother desires that one of her sons shall take and keep the yellow robe, yet the younger among the educated Burmese are frank in calling the order of monks a " yellow peril," not because they are bad men, for public opinion in Burma rarely tolerates immorality in these religious leaders, but because there are so many of them, over seventy-five thousand in the whole country. To feed such a horde of mendicants is a costly business, and the rebuilding and gilding of a pagoda may mean that the inheritance of every one belonging to its village will be decimated. " The pagoda is built and the village ruined," they ruefully repeat. Thus there is growing up among those who are in the government schools in contact with the liberal thinking of the West a disposition to question the values of the present religious system. Possibly not more than ten per cent. of the students who have Western training can be called orthodox Buddhists. Thus the old people to whom Buddhism means so much are anxious, and the young are restive. Burma, like many other countries, is going through a period of transition, the outcome of which is uncertain. Yet undoubtedly it is still a strongly Buddhist country, and the masses of its people are not much affected by this spirit of scepticism. As, however, Western education is the key to preferment the official classes are apt to sit loose to much that their fathers held sacred. And some few are busy re-thinking their faith and seeking to adapt it to modern needs.

(e) *The Better Side of Burmese Buddhism.*—Buddhism is often described as a pessimistic religion. As one sees it in Burma, however, it seems to make the people happy and contented. Possibly this is due to their naturally cheerful temperament. Whatever the reason, there is a remarkable joyousness about the gay-robed crowds of happy, smiling people.

Again, while Buddhism does not give to womanhood nearly so high a place as does the religion of Jesus, yet it has granted her a far better standing than she has in any part of India under Hinduism or Islam. Woman is the "better half" in Burma and knows it, even though she may pray to be born next as a man.

Caste, moreover, the great bane of India, is almost unknown to Buddhist Burma: it is a cheerful democratic land. Buddhism believes in the education of the masses, and its schools and monasteries are open to all. It is also very tolerant and kindly. It has not led on any large scale either to religious persecution or to war. These are no small services. Moreover, Buddhism has in the past been a great bond of union between the peoples of Asia, and it is to-day again playing some part in the movement, "Asia for the Asiatics"—a movement deserving our sympathetic attention. In the great awakening of Nationalism the Buddhist Revival has its share both as cause and as effect.

3. Prospects of Christianity in Burma.

There are only some twenty thousand Burmese Christians as yet, although, within the confines of Burma there is a far larger number of Christians, and the Karens are already a great church. What, then, are the reasons for confidence that Burma will at some time be a Christian country, albeit with a Christianity whose type will differ very greatly from the prevailing types of the West?

(a) *The Burmese are truly Religious in Temperament.*—The natural instinct of the Burmese for religion is strong. They are not content with mere ritual and with offerings, lavish as these are. Gratitude to Gotama, the great Teacher and lord of life, is a real motive to many. Not uncommonly are Christian hymns adapted by modern educated Buddhists and sung in honour of the Buddha:

> "Glory, laud and honour
> To our Lord and King,
> This through countless ages,
> Men and Devas sing."

These Buddhists have organised Buddhist Sunday Schools. In these the children not only closely imitate Protestant Sunday Schools but sing to a small portable harmonium :

> " Buddha loves me, this I know ;
> For the Scriptures tell me so,"

or more usually Burmese hymns and " carols."

(b) *They tend to view Gotama as a Saviour.*—Again many look upon Gotama as a loving saviour. So strong is this attitude toward him that when a father blesses his child, he says to him : " May you be reborn when the Loving One, *Metteya*,* comes." Gotama is reported as having promised the coming of such a redeemer. Even in Southern Asia, therefore, Buddhism is changing from a way of merit and self-mastery into a way of salvation by faith. May we not reckon this transition as a preparation for the message of Christianity ? Buddhism everywhere is to-day almost more like Christianity than it is like the Buddhism of Gotama and the Elders. The Buddhism of Burma is more of a religion and less of a philosophy than that of the Books.

(c) *The Christian Heaven is more Attractive than Nibbāna.*—It is clear again that Buddhists to-day are much more ready than before to accept the idea of a Christian heaven. This heaven, preached as a state of progress, a meeting-place of friends, and the beatific vision of God, is very attractive to them. The appeal of *Nibbāna* is dying: "*Nibbāna,*" said a monk in Burma, "is a fearsome thought. I have no hope of attaining it." "We are walking in

* Sanskrit, *Maitri*.

darkness," said another leader, "without seeing a light, a person, or a hope."

Missionaries both in Burma and Ceylon are agreed that the teaching of Buddhism has changed very greatly during the last few decades, among those who have come directly or indirectly in touch with Christianity. Formerly Buddhists preached that there was no supreme god, that *Nibbāna* meant total quiescence, almost total annihilation, that man is his own saviour, and that there is no possible escape from the penalty of sin; now many admit that there must be a God, declare that Gotama is a saviour, that sin is forgiven and that there is a heaven in place of *Nibbāna*.

On the other hand, there is still much work for the Christian missionary. Buddhism in many parts of Burma seems to be making one great last stand against the gospel of Christ. Its own standard is in many respects so high that our Christianity is as a whole not loving or sacrificial enough to win its adherents. The Christianity which is to be an overpowering argument for the efficacy and truth of the Christian faith is too rare. The Buddhist Revival is largely a reaction from our Western pseudo-Christianity, and from the shameless aggression of Christendom.

(d) *Moral Conditions Demand a Vital Christianity.*—The moral situation in Burma clearly demands that either a revivified Buddhism or Christianity in its most vital form should come to the rescue. The need is grave. Burma is at once the most literate and the most criminal portion of the Indian Empire. A government report for 1912 reads: "The moral sense of the people is diminishing with a slackening of religious observances. With the decay of ancient beliefs the Buddhist religion is losing its moral sanction as an inspiring force in the lives of its adherents. Drunkenness, gambling, drug-taking and vicious habits, increasing as they all are, tend to produce a weakening of self-control and a loss of self-respect which in favouring circumstances easily create the criminal." A fair-minded missionary would agree that these deplorable conditions are in large measure chargeable to the impact of Western "civilisation." It is incumbent upon us, in ordinary justice and fair play, to see that the West is represented by our very best men in missionary service, in commerce and in government posts. On the other hand, these deplorable moral conditions are also due to the fact that Buddhism has not succeeded in its task of building character. A genuine and vital Christianity has a large and hopeful task in Burma. These very attractive people need a dynamic and a bond of union in great enterprises. They are seeking such a religion.

(e) *Loving Social Service finds its own Way to the Heart.*—When Christianity is expressed in deeds of loving social service, such as work for lepers, for the deaf and the blind, or for any other needy class in the community, it touches a responsive chord in every Buddhist heart. They subscribe to our Christian mission work for the afflicted. The social appeal of Christianity will go far toward breaking down all forms of prejudice: and it is significant that the young Burmese are organising their own Y.M.B.A.'s and their own social service clubs, though at present these movements do not exhibit much staying-power.

(f) *Christianity dispels the Fear of the Demon World.*—Christianity reveals its power by dispelling the terrors of demon-haunted villages, and lessening the horrors of the slums of the great cities. A country like Burma is not interested in a new system of ethics. It is wholly satisfied with the admirable system it already possesses. But it does welcome the sense of spiritual freedom and power which Christianity can impart. "The kingdom of God is not in word, but in power." May we not say that Christ can give strength to follow the Noble Path of which Gotama spoke?

II. BUDDHISM IN CEYLON

1. On a Hillside near Kandy.

Over against this sketch of Buddhism as it appears in Burma let us consider a scene in a neighbouring land, the island of Ceylon, where for twenty-five hundred years, the religion of the yellow robe has held almost undisputed sway. Here it has a supreme opportunity, and has often used it nobly, building a great civilisation for a thousand years.

It is early spring. The rains are over, and in the brilliant moonlight, the Singhalese peasants have gathered from their little malarial villages to listen to *bana*, the preaching of the Buddhist Law.

(a) *The Dullness and Superstition of Village Life in Southern Ceylon.*—Life is dull in these villages, and any incident and any teaching will be welcome. It is a strange world in which these people live, "a world of bare and brutal facts; of superstition, of grotesque imagination ; a world of hunger and fear and devils, where a man is helpless before the unseen, unintelligible forces surrounding him." As in Burma, so in Ceylon, demonism is inextricably interwoven with the Buddhism of the people. In Ceylon, however, it is a darker and more sinister demonism, blending with a far more sombre and pessimistic Buddhism. Devils and anti-devils, exorcists and monks, incantations and prayers to Buddha mingle in the dim confused minds of these poor Kandyan villagers. It is not very long since human sacrifices were made to the " demons " of disease.

(b) *The Themes of the Hillside Preacher.*—This darker pessimism speaks through the monotonous sing-song of the yellow-robed monk on the hillside, as he speaks to the villagers, urging upon them that life is transient and full of sorrow, that none the less their chief duty is to avoid taking the life of the meanest animal, not even killing the malarial mosquito or the plague-bringing rat against which government edicts have gone out. Here religion is in conflict with science and with family love : which is to die, my child or the rat ? There can in the end of the day be but one answer.

(c) *The Stolidity of his Audience.*—The men listen dully, chewing their betel-nut. They have not much use for the monks, who own one-third of the arable land of the country and are a heavy drain upon its resources. Except fitfully, they are not schoolmasters like those of Burma, but tend to be drones in the hive. When they do teach the children they only emphasise the doctrines of rebirth and of not-killing ; yet some are kind and teach reading and writing to the little ones. And occasionally one leads a life of such real piety as to justify this division of labour—" the people to work, the monk to meditate." But saints are rare in all lands.

2. The Hold of Buddhism upon the Singhalese.

Even in this village audience, crude as the preaching and dull as the response to it may be, there is a certain sense of religious peace, of an otherworldly calm. The *Dharma* has not lost its power. What are the deep roots which the great tree of Buddhism has put out in the island of Ceylon? Of these the more intelligent Buddhist laity will speak. Let us question this young lawyer, dressed in Western style, who stands looking on with some contempt.

(a) *Appeal of its Traditions.*—Such men are impressed by what they see of a very ancient and very real civilisation, which Buddhism undoubtedly built. In the jungles everywhere are the remains of the days when Buddhism taught the people to irrigate their fields, to build strong cities, to write remarkable books, and to develop a genuine culture. The ruined cities of Anuradhapura and Pollanaruwa, in spite of the incursions of the jungle and of the neglect of centuries, are still magnificent and eloquent monuments of what was a really great civilisation when Europe was still barbarian. Here the patriot sees the melancholy remnants of a great Buddhist nation, great not only in the beauty of its art, but great in the tanks and irrigation systems now almost hidden by rank undergrowth, but remaining to prove that the whole of this vast deserted area was once under cultivation. Great, too, was the spirit of some of these rulers. Imagine the emotions which surge in the young patriot's heart as he thinks of all the devastation caused by the great European war and then stands before the calm statue of the noble Dutu Gemunu who to save his people from war, sought out the invader and slew him in single combat, and then in the greatness of his heart put up a splendid monument in his honour! It is on account of such things as these that the young modern Singhalese is convinced that Buddhism has still a place in the world.

Wave after wave of European aggression has swept over Ceylon, arousing a resentment which leads the Singhalese even to exaggerate the glories of ancient Buddhism. It is not strange that they do so. Moreover, although it is fashionable in Ceylon to despise the mendicants of the yellow robe, the fact that there are still about eight thousand monks shows that in these days of disillusionment there are many world-weary men, to whom the traditional attraction of the monastic life is overpoweringly strong and who find under it protection and peace. I have seen strong and true boys being drawn under its spell, and have known some noble characters among the monks.

(b) *Its work of Reformation.*—The intelligent Buddhist layman emphasises not merely the sense of peace and quiet satisfaction which Buddhism affords; he also claims that it has done away with caste and has purified religion. He will often compare the dignity, the stately beauty, and the harmlessness of the Buddhist temple and its surroundings with the incredibly gross indecencies of a Saivite shrine in Southern India. Men must worship something: in Buddhism they worship a good and great man deified. In Saivite Hinduism they mingle the base passions of a perverted sexuality with their worship.

(c) *Its Leadership of Public Opinion.*—This apologist argues, too, that Buddhism still retains the power of moulding public opinion. He instances the strenuous appeals which the Buddhists have made to the Ceylon government to suppress instead of encourage the liquor traffic: and points to some of their good schools, where young Ceylon is being taught the great moral lessons of their Faith. And though Theosophists from the West have been most responsible for starting these, the Buddhists keep them up and are adding new buildings and improving their quality.

(d) *Yet Ceylon needs Christianity.*—It is clear that much as Buddhism has done for this lovely land, it does need Jesus Christ—as indeed all lands, not least our own, need Him—in increasing measure as they face the complexities of the modern world.

He is needed in jungle village and in teeming city, to cast out fear and sin, and to enable His people to live nearer to their ideals. They, too, have gifts for Him! And we and they are partners in a glorious enterprise: to establish His Kingdom of Love and Truth in all the world. Their devotion to their Buddha, no less than their need and helplessness to-day, is an inspiring motive to the Christian missionary to win them to Christ.

3. Two Sharply Marked Attitudes among Buddhists.

Let us return to the hillside preacher. A change has come over his audience. All are now alert and eager. Seated around his platform, they are holding a cord which seems to bind them in some mystic circle. It is "*Pirit*"; a kind of magic incantation. The preacher is reciting the ancient runes by which evil is averted and demon armies kept at bay. He is telling how the bandit, Angulimāla, who had killed nine hundred and ninety-nine victims and wore their fingers as a chaplet, tried to kill the Buddha so as to make the full tale of a thousand, but was converted on the spot. "May the merit of this be yours," he says, and they all cry, "*Sadhu,* Amen."

"All humbug," grunts the layman. "Come, let us go to the Young Men's Buddhist Association, where a Singhalese advocate, newly returned from England, is going to read a paper on 'Buddhism, a Gospel for Europe.'" Leaving the palms and fragrant trees of the jungle silhouetted against the brilliant sky, and passing the white buildings of the Buddhist High School and of the precious and venerated Temple of the Tooth, he talks of this possibility. It seems that a movement is on foot to send a mission to Europe. We agree that, if Christians were real followers of Jesus of Nazareth, such missions would be futile: and that the spirit of Gotama is akin to that of Jesus. "We see your Christ," he says; "in His beauty, because we have first seen the beauty of our Buddha." Here is a preparation for the gospel indeed. And may not all idealists—Christians, Buddhists, and others—co-operate much more freely than they do in great causes? In a League of Nations, for example, and in social programmes? In Ceylon, as in Burma, Buddhism is in some degree adapting itself to the new world-environment. Its old cry of pain,

"All is fleeting, transient, sorrowful," is giving place to attempts at social service and positive living. Yet as compared with Burma or with Christian lands, the predominating note among Buddhists in Ceylon is one of world-weariness and despair.

III. BUDDHISM IN SIAM

1. Siam a Buddhist Kingdom.

Ceylon and Burma were for many centuries Buddhist kingdoms with a sovereign as patron and supporter of the monks and very often with members of the royal family amongst the great abbots. Buddhism has indeed depended much upon royal patronage, and in these days when kings are rare it is of special interest to get a glimpse of a modern Buddhist kingdom which is not unlike those of the past. Let us study a great festival in Siam where the king's own brother is Head of the Order and where he himself is a staunch patron of Buddhism.

2. The Thot Krathin Festival.

Some time between the eleventh and twelfth moons his majesty visits the temples round Bangkok which are under his royal patronage. For weeks past every household in Siam, from that of the King to that of the poorest peasant, has been busy "laying down holy cloth" or making patchwork robes for the monks, that the letter of the old commandment "be ye clothed in rags" may be observed, and the monks be supplied with their year's clothing.

At the same time offerings of bedding, furniture, and food are made and great merit is acquired by the faithful. The King in his splendid barge of state, with its prows shaped like dragons, its sixty oarsmen, its canopy of cloth of gold, sets out for one of the great *Wats* or temples; he is seated on his throne, and wears a golden crown, and about him are numerous little princes. Arrived at the shrine his retainers carry the bales of cloth and other offerings into the temple, and then the King himself with due ceremony and amidst barbaric music and military salutes, comes down from the barge and lights five candles which stand upon the table prepared for his offering. Then, burning incense, he bows to the image of the Buddha, to the sacred books written on strips of palm-leaf, and to the Order of Monks; he is "taking refuge" in the Buddhist Jewels. He then reverently asks the abbot to accept him as a lay-adherent, and to allow him to keep the Five Precepts, not to kill, not to steal, not to commit sexual sin, not to lie nor to drink strong drink. And if it be a holy day he will also take the vows of a monk, not to eat after midday, not to watch theatrical shows, nor use perfumes, nor sleep on a high luxurious bed. Then as he offers his gifts the monks accept them, crying "*Sadhu*" (Amen or well done), and distribution is made according to their rank. So amidst their blessings he bows again to the Three Jewels and makes a solemn departure to another shrine.

3. The King and Pāli Learning.

The present King, whom we may call for short King Mahamongkut (he has more names than the

Hohenzollerns), is a graduate of Oxford, a man of the world, and a great patron of Buddhist scholarship. This has been a tradition of his house for centuries and in no small degree the present interest in Pāli learning in Western countries is due to the enthusiasm of the ruling house of Siam, which has presented splendid libraries of the sacred books to many universities and temples. The King summons the monkish candidates for degrees in Pāli learning to undergo examinations every three years; and for nine days in the comparatively cool weather of the early part of the year makes a royal festival in their honour, during which they are undergoing an examination which increases every day in stiffness. Those who survive to the end are given the degree *Pareean ek*, or "first-class honours," and with it goes a small pension; those who drop out before the end are given second-, third-, or fourth-class degrees. So the knowledge of the sacred books is kept alive and some of these Siamese scholars reach a remarkable degree of proficiency. Their influence has been potent in a renaissance of Pāli learning in Burma and Ceylon.

4. Buddhist Education.

In Siam as in Burma the monks are the elementary schoolmasters. The boys all spend some time as novices, during which they not only learn the rudiments of the religion but reading, writing, and arithmetic. As in Burma, very little is done for the education of the girls, though this is steadily improving owing to the splendid work done by mission schools.

5. The Temples or Wats.

These Siamese pagodas, fantastic and gay with gold and sky-blue tiles, are of four grades, those built by the King and dedicated to him, those built by the princes, those built by the nobles, and lastly those built by the common people, usually by subscription organised by the monks or by some enthusiastic laymen. Merit gained in this and similar ways has been called "The Sum and Substance of Siamese Buddhism": there is some truth in these generalisations as regards the whole of Southern Asia. But in Siam as elsewhere there is genuine devotion to the religion of Buddha, and the human heart is not as calculating as this sentence implies. Moreover, there is considerable attempt to modernise the religion to fit the new age, and many of the people follow the King in believing that it can be made the basis for a modern state, and can unify and uplift the peoples. All that helps to build up a nation is welcomed in Siam, and Christianity therefore has an open door here as in Ceylon and Burma. Burma is tolerant, but Siam desires the friendship of Western peoples, and being independent is freer to develop along its own lines. Let us now attempt to summarise our impressions of the Buddhism of these lands of Southern Asia by describing other typical scenes in each.

IV. SOME TYPES OF BUDDHIST RELIGIOUS LIFE

1. The Cremation of a Singhalese Abbot.

A great Singhalese abbot has passed away. It is a national event. The hillside near Kandy is thronged with great companies of monks in every shade of yellow and brown, while around them surges a sombre sea of the faithful laity. In the centre of the huge assemblage is the funeral-pyre, draped in white and red. Standing beside it, a monk is telling in solemn and mournful tones of the greatness and goodness of the departed, who, though he had not become worthy of *Nibbāna*, had his feet surely set upon the upward path leading to a good rebirth in *so-wan*, a heaven. Then amidst solemn chanting and the wailing of flutes and throbbing of drums he applies a torch to the pyre. While the people bow their heads and cry "*sadhu*" (Amen), the body turns to ashes. Then solemnly and silently the great throng disperses, the lay people to take up the ordinary duties of life, the monks to meditate upon its transient character and unreality. And here a young novice, to whom the dead man has been very dear, stays weeping, until the last embers die down and night comes swiftly on.

2. The Funeral Rites of a Burmese Monk.

Another funeral scene. It is that of a Buddhist monk in Burma—a *Hpongyi*. The whole country-side is present. In clothing of exquisite silk, resembling a brilliant swarm of butterflies, the people surround the great catafalque, blazing with tinsel and gold leaf, on which lies the embalmed body of the monk. After a time the coffin is taken down and a programme of merry-making begins. The young bloods of the village to which the monk has belonged, range themselves in two carefully picked teams on either side of it. Then begins a tug-of-war with the body in its coffin, the victorious team treating the defeated to drinks, and to side shows at the little booths which cluster round, awaiting custom. These and other contests make a glad and joyful scene at which all the people rejoice, for has not the good man been released from this transient life (which, nevertheless, is good and satisfying while blood is hot and youth endures)? Has he not returned to a life of glory, and won much merit for his own folk and for all the faithful?

In due time the body is restored to its resting place on the funeral pyre, the fire is lighted, and the whole mass flares up in flame and smoke, consuming not only the body, but along with it the decorations, including paintings of numerous demons, among whom may be an Englishman with a gun! Only demons could kill for sport! When it is consumed, the crowd disperses with shouts of merriment, well content, not least among the others the relatives of the departed. A good show has been staged, the dead has been honoured, the family name has been distinguished, and everybody is satisfied. If for the next year or more the family exchequer has been sorely depleted, still "it is the custom," and every one expects to follow it. Some one has well said that Buddhism in Burma is a cheery and social affair, "from festive marriages to no less festive funerals." I confess to an admiration for this cheerful view of death, even if some of its expressions are bizarre! It is less pagan than our "blacks, and funeral obsequies."

3. A Similar Scene in Siam.

The Funeral of a Siamese Prince.—A nephew of the King has died, and his funeral sermon is being preached by another royal Prince, who is also a monk, and who is true to type and to the orthodox Buddhism of his race. "As kinsmen welcome kinsmen returning after long sojourn in far countries, so do good deeds welcome the good as they enter the other world. And what are good deeds, but the unselfish effort to advance the good of others? All must be left behind as we enter the Gate of Death; but as a shadow follows the body so do purity and simplicity of heart and deed steal after us, and minister to us in that world beyond. As a flame is our mortal life, and if there be no fuel it burns no more. We know not when it may die down, for all that has a beginning has also an end, and transient are all things. And as we may take with us only virtue, shall we not cherish and ensue it?"

We are reminded of the picture by G. F. Watts, "*Sic Transit Gloria Mundi,*" in which another prince is seen upon the bier, his crown, his books, his winecup laid aside; and over his bier are the words, "What I spent I had, what I had I lost, what I gave I have." It is sound Buddhism, and every word of this sermon of the royal monk is drawn from the *Dhammapada*, accepted in all Buddhist lands as the very words of the Buddha, himself the prototype of a long line of kings and princes in many lands, who have been proud to wear the Yellow Robe.

4. The Secret of Buddhism's Influence.

Which of these funeral scenes (chosen because Buddhism plays almost its chief part at such times) is most true to type? It is a perplexing question. Buddhism has from the very beginning been chiefly a religion for monks, calling men and women to leave the world. It was never exactly optimistic, and yet another permanent root of its remarkable power over humankind has been that often men and women who obeyed possessed a sense of discovery, of hopefulness, of sheer joy; especially strong in its golden age, the first five centuries of its existence. There was something vernal in the air. "In joy we live, hating none; let us live in the midst of those who hate, unhating; in the midst of those who ail, let us live in perfect health; having nothing, yet we possess great riches." Such is the spirit of the early *sangha* (monastic community). And when we turn to the Buddhism of to-day we find that it retains these two dominant characteristics: this blending of sadness and quiet joy. Even in sunny Burma the old people and the monks seem sad at times, and even in Ceylon and Siam the ordinary folk are fairly cheerful as they go on pilgrimages or make their offerings to monk or image.

V. BUDDHISM AS A LIVING RELIGION

Buddhism stands in a different relation to Christianity from any other world religion, because it has unquestionably done for Eastern peoples something of the intellectual, moral, and spiritual service which Christianity has done for Europe and America. Moreover, it is showing a strange power of revival. It also seems to make a real appeal to certain types of mind in the West. Little groups of Westerners in Burma and in Ceylon, the former Scotch, the latter German, have for some years been promoting the propagation of Buddhism in Western lands. They feel convinced that it is " the religion of mature minds." One of their number, a Scot, known as *Bhikkhu Silācāra*,* wrote in 1913: " This seems to be the place of honour which Burma is called upon to fill in the family of the nations of the world—that of being *Dhammadāyaka* to the world, giver of the *dhamma* † of the Blessed One to all the nations of the earth. What prouder, what more glorious, what more merit-bringing position could any people ask for than to be chosen as the bearer of the sublime teaching of the Blessed One? " There is a considerable amount of publication of Buddhist propaganda to-day in Europe and America, even if few Eastern Buddhists are found with the courage to preach Buddhism in person in Western cities. In Germany, where there are said to be scores of thousands of Buddhists, a publishing house

* Sanskrit, *Bhikshu*. It means "mendicant."
† *Dhamma* means " law " or " teaching."

has been set up at Breslau; and the *Buddhist Review* is published in London. In North America Buddhism has numerous missions, especially on the Pacific Coast, where it aims at converting Americans as well as at ministering to the Japanese. It is the only non-Christian religion which has this appeal. What gives it this hold, not only upon great sections of the East, but also upon those who have been born within the range of Christianity, is a question which needs a thoughtful answer. It is a question of vital importance to us all.

1. It takes hold where Faith in Christianity has ceased.

Buddhism makes a strong appeal to minds dissatisfied with Christianity, or unwilling to accept the claims of Christ. It is not difficult to draw analogies between the acts and sayings of Jesus and those of Gotama. It is easy to be enthusiastic over the ethical teachings of Buddhism, and over its great influence upon Asia. It has a certain appeal too to the scientific mind, which is not found in any other non-Christian religion; and some claim that it is more satisfying to the intellect than Christianity. The appeal of Buddhism, therefore, is more than a mild satisfaction of curiosity in something novel; it gives to a mind which denies the fundamentals of Christianity an apparently good religious substitute. This being true, no one can question the fact that those who are to go as Christian missionaries to Buddhist countries must take the utmost pains to prepare themselves to meet those who believe in Buddhism, not merely with friendliness and a sense of sympathy, but with an adequate background of philosophical, psychological, and religious training which enables them adequately to represent the best that is in Christianity, and to deal sympathetically and fairly with Buddhism at its best. Missionaries are all too few who can " out-think " these Scotch and German Buddhists, who carry much influence with the peoples among whom they live. Some of them are sincere and able men : and there are also strong native defenders of the Buddhist Faith. Moreover, without a deep appreciation of the power of Buddhism one cannot understand the history and culture of Asia. And this study becomes daily more important and more interesting.

2. It faces the Fact of Suffering.

Where shall one begin in his endeavour to grasp the essential teachings of Buddhism? No one can fully understand Buddhism without studying Hinduism as a background and starting point. The student can go far, however, by starting from the fact of universal human suffering, and its relief. " One thing only do I teach," said Buddha, " sorrow and the uprooting of sorrow." He was never weary of bringing home to his disciples the horror of the world's pain, in order that he might lead them on to what he believed to be the only way of salvation. " What think ye, O monks, which is vaster, the flood of tears that, weeping and lamenting, ye in your past lives have shed, or the waters of the four great oceans? Long time, O monks, have ye suffered the death of father, mother, brothers, and sisters. Long time have ye undergone the loss of your goods; long time have ye been afflicted with sickness, old age, and death." "Where is the joy, where is the laughter, when all is in flames about us?" Buddhism is often labelled pessimistic, because its writings are full of attempts, such as these, to make men realise the suffering and the worthlessness of the life to which they cling. The critics, however, do not realise the hopes which it holds out to a suffering world, which are just as characteristic of Buddhistic teaching. The Buddhist replies, "If medical science is pessimistic then Buddhism is also pessimistic." It diagnoses the disease in order to cure it.

Like other religions it is a "Way out." It first states the problem: then offers a solution.

3. It affords a Way of Escape from Sorrow.

In India Gotama had an easier task than he would have faced in the full-blooded and less thoughtful West. We Westerners do not need to be convinced of the pain of life, we are now wide awake to it; but to the Hindu of the sixth century before Christ a conviction of the emptiness of life was something in the nature of an obsession. The bright, naïve optimism of earlier ages, revealed, for example, in the *Rig-Veda*,* had passed away; a combination of circumstances, climate, speculative activities, disappointments and other causes, had combined to make India pessimistic. Chief of these causes was undoubtedly the belief in transmigration which has come more and more to occupy a central

* The *Rig-Veda* is a great anthology of religion. The Vedas are early religious Books in which a joyous nature-worship predominates.

position in Hinduism. It represents man as doomed to wander from birth to birth, and to expiate every deed of his past. It is impossible for us in the West to realise how firm a hold this thought has upon India, or how great is the longing for a way of escape. Gotama's resolute attempt to find such a way of escape, his assurance that he had discovered it, and his enthusiastic preaching of "the Way" brought Buddhism into the world as a new religion, and became a veritable "gospel" to weary and jaded hearts.

4. It is a Practical Creed: Its Founder called Himself "A Physician of Sick Souls."

Born the son of a chieftain in Nepal in the foothills of the Himalayas, about 560 B.C., Gotama, the great founder of Buddhism, was sheltered from the sights and sounds of suffering, as we are told in the loving stories of Buddhist lore, until the gods, who had a higher destiny in store for him than that of an Indian princeling, revealed to him the facts of old age and decay and death. In a series of visions—of the old man tottering down to the grave, of the leper riddled with foul disease, of the corpse laid out for the burning, the great fact of human suffering came home to him. It made so deep an impression that he renounced his royal rights and went out as a mendicant ascetic to discover some way of escape. He was then twenty-nine years old. Not until he had reached the age of thirty-eight, and had honestly tried the various accepted paths for the attainment of holiness and the escape from the burdens of life laid down by Hindu sages, did he find what he was seeking. Sitting under the Indian fig-tree in the heat of the day, he meditated patiently and long until the vision dawned upon him, or, as we should say, until his sub-consciousness, which had long been working upon the problem presented to it, sent a complete and satisfying solution into the focus of his conscious mind. His solution, recognising the fact that Hindu practices had vainly attempted to drug the aching nerve of pain or to tear it out, offered a more positive remedy. The present writer believes that the Spirit of God had much to do with this discovery. There are, however, among missionaries, many who feel that this is a grievous heresy, and are bitterly opposed to any such view.

In order to understand the solution which Gotama offered to the world, which undoubtedly captured the enthusiasm of unnumbered millions of weary pilgrims in India and other lands, it may be well to consider Gotama's own description of himself as "a physician of sick souls." Just as the physician must first diagnose the disease and recognise the germ which is its secret cause, before he can give the right treatment, so Gotama set himself to discover the hidden cause of the world's suffering. He thought that he had found it in that universal clinging to life which he called *tanhā*, which means a "craving" for anything less austere than *Nibbanā*. "From *tanhā* springs sorrow; he that is free from *tanhā* is freed from sorrow and suffering."

This is the source of all the world's agony, says Gotama: and if we face the facts we shall see that egoism of men and nations, a form of *tanhā*, accounts for most of it! The modern world is full of *tanhā*.

5. It cultivates a Sense of the Worthlessness of Temporal Things.

It is because man clings to things which cannot fully satisfy him, such as the love of family, the desire for wealth and fame, the wish to be reborn in a heaven (all of which are classed together in Buddhism), that he has to go on being reborn. This is the Buddhist doctrine of *Kamma*. Hinduism, like much orthodox Christianity, thinks of a " soul " which dwells in the body. The Hindu thinks of it as passing from one body to another in the process of transmigration. The view of Buddhism is rather that the " ego " of man is a stream of mental energy, the direction of which is under his own control. If he dies full of *tanhā*, cleaving to the things of this world, he will surely be reborn to some sort of misery. If, on the other hand, he dies detached from human interests and open-eyed to the worthlessness of temporal things, he will eventually be set free from the entanglement of life, as we know it on earth, and will pass into *Nibbāna*. Of this goal one can only say with assurance that it is unlike anything known to mortal man,* and that its essence is moral purity.

6. Its Conception of Bliss is realisable in this Life.

But Gotama was not concerned with the next life so much as with this. He laid emphasis also

* *Nirvāna* means to the Hindu reabsorption into the Absolute *Brahman*. To Buddhists it is variously expounded by their teachers as either (*a*) annihilation, or (*b*) a heaven of bliss, or (*c*) annihilation of evil desire, *i.e.* of all clinging to life. Western Buddhist writers call it usually by some such phrase as " The great Peace," which is vague enough to mean any of the three !

upon the wonderful joy and peace which the fixed purpose to achieve *Nibbāna* had caused him to experience. This was the real relief from suffering, which he had in mind. "Whoso is pure from all *tanhā*, he is in *Nibbāna*." This he preached with great conviction and enthusiasm, declaring that men might aim in this life to attain the position of an *arhat* (saint) and actually enter into the preliminary experience of *Nibbāna*. It is this aspect of Buddhism which makes it a true religion. Its joy and power can be experienced in the midst of the world's pain. So it is called an "Island," a "Refuge," where the drowning man may escape, or a "Cool Retreat," whither one may fly from a world in flames.

7. Buddhism is a Religion of Enlightenment and Reason.

Buddhism exhibits salvation as, first of all, a way of understanding. It is a religion of analysis, which bids man see life steadily and see it whole, by first taking it to pieces! When one looks at the body, what is it, says Buddhism, after all, that we should regard ourselves as attached to it? There are so many bones, so many tendons, so much skin, so many juices. If a man views the body with an anatomical eye, he will see it as it really is; disgust will arise in him which will lead him out into detachment. A Buddhist is sometimes urged to practise the habit of sitting in cemeteries or among reminders of the dead, or to have a skeleton near at hand, in order that he may meditate upon the transient nature of all that is mortal. Similarly he is to dispel anger or lust by asking, "Who is it I am angry with, after whom do I lust, but a bag of bones?" It seeks to dispel passion by reason.

8. It has a strong Moral Code: The "Four Noble Truths," and the "Eight-fold Path."

As the old Teacher was passing away he emphasised anew the part which intelligent belief plays in the Buddhist scheme of religion. "It is through not understanding and not grasping four things, O monks, that we have to abide and wander through this maze of being," he remarked. The four things which he had in mind were suffering, its real cause (*tanhā*), the cure of suffering, and the path which leads to *Nibbāna*. These are the "Four Noble Truths" of Buddhism, driven home to every disciple as the very foundation of his religious life.

With reference to the "way" which leads to *Nibbāna* Buddhism has made its most remarkable contribution to human thought. It is called the "Middle Way," between the extremes of an austere asceticism and a spirit of worldliness, a clear-cut and admirably arranged ethical scheme, which has undoubtedly done much to elevate the nations among whom it has been practised. The "eight practices," urged upon every one who aspires to spiritual growth, are right thinking (about the "four noble truths," etc.), right aspirations (benevolence, pity, brotherhood, etc.), right speech, right action, right livelihood (by industries which are not harmful), right effort of mind, right attention (alertness), and right contemplation, or mystic meditation. Such a scheme may readily be ritualised and deadened, but it lends itself no less readily to the cultivation of simple virtues. A popular summary, universally known, teaches "Do good, shun ill, and cleanse the inmost thoughts, this is the teaching of Buddhas."

The "eight-fold path" is usually developed under three main endeavours—enlightenment, morality, and concentrated meditation. Stage by stage the disciple is led along this path. "Step by step, day by day, one may purify one's heart from defilements by understanding, even as the smith purifies silver in the fire." The true disciple must avoid the extremes of asceticism, on the one hand, or of entanglement with the world on the other. So the noble path claims to be a "middle path" of sweet reasonableness. The lines are not always clearly drawn between ritual offences or mistakes and moral failures, and the ideal life often seems to be represented as primarily monastic, but there is no doubt that one who deliberately sets himself to follow the "eight-fold path" would be a lovable and strong type of character, something like the fine old monk from Tibet in Kipling's "Kim." And there have been many such, men not only of his gentle strength, but men filled with missionary zeal and devotion to noble tasks.

9. It has come to practise Prayer.

In spite of the protests of Gotama against attempts to persuade the gods, this is what most Buddhists in Southern Asia have come to do: and in Tibet, China, and Japan prayer is multiplied by mechanical devices, such as prayer-wheels, prayer-cylinders, and prayer-flags — a degeneration of mysticism into magic, not unknown in some Christian lands. The human heart is hungry and wants to pray! And even this religion of enlightenment and of the fixed causality of the universe has had to find a place for prayer. And

Divine Beings have been called in to answer the aspiration of the heart. Gotama himself is deified: and folk pray to him in Burma, Siam, and Ceylon: whilst in the other Buddhist lands they have learnt to love such compassionate beings as Kwanyin, and Amitābha, Buddha of eternal Light who saves men by his grace. That there is mercy in heaven is the hope of every man. It is but a pathetic dream, until we know that the heavens have spoken and declared that mercy in the Word made Flesh.

"So through the thunder comes a human voice."

10. Yet it emphasises Stoical Self-mastery.

On the other hand, the whole trend of early Buddhism is stoical. It sets up a lofty moral ideal, yet offers relatively little assistance in attaining it. Admiration for the Buddha, faith in the system he preached, common-sense or enlightened self-interest in accepting the great truth that happiness follows upon goodness—these furnish the motive power of a Buddhist religious life. In theory, at least, there is no god higher than the little local deities who are said to have bowed down before the Buddha. Inasmuch, moreover, as they are also subject to *kamma*, the gods are less admirable and less helpful than he. To some thinkers this stoical self-mastery is the strongest element of Buddhism. "I am the captain of my soul," a good Buddhist would say: "I am the master of my fate." But to those who think more deeply, this will appear an element of weakness, for everywhere and in all ages the human heart finds no ultimate satisfaction without a belief in some loftier, purer, and stronger Being, who is ready to hear and to help. And in the more developed Buddhism of the North such theology plays a very great part. The history of Buddhism is one of the best chapters in Christian apologetics and deserves close study. As we shall see, the Japanese Buddhist believes in a Trinitarian theology, and in an evangelical doctrine of salvation: and, in one great sect, has urged its priests to marry.

11. It has Two Standards of Morality.

A very serious defect of Southern Buddhism is its double standard of morality, one for the layman and another for the monk. It places the celibate *bhikkhu* (mendicant) on a higher footing than the layman. During the Buddha's own lifetime he was accused of making many homes desolate, and this has been a constant criticism in China where it is a crime not to beget sons; and where Buddhism has been obstinately monastic. There have been great exceptions, especially where kings have been good Buddhists, but it is on the whole a monastic religion, and has continually reverted to type.

12. It rates Womanhood Low.

Another alleged weakness, which will specially interest those who are entering upon the careful study of non-Christian religions at the present time, is the relatively low place which the Buddhist system, at least in theory, gives to women. While in practice, as has been pointed out, the women of Burma are the better half of the population, yet in strict theory they are not "human beings" at all: they are less than human: only he who takes the yellow robe and becomes for a time a monk reaches the status of full humanity. Yet Gotama said equally severe things about men; the two sexes, he taught, are a snare to one another: but women are the worse! A Singhalese Christian pastor praying for power to resist the Devil added, "and all *her* works," and women are in fact so described in many passages of the Buddhist Books. Love between the sexes and lust are not distinguished. And here, perhaps, is the supreme service that Jesus renders to human society: he makes family life a sacred thing, and safeguards women and children from abuse, bringing them to honour and sanctity. Buddhism being concerned chiefly with the monastic life of meditation has not much to say about the family. It does not, at least in Southern Asia, teach the Fatherhood of God from whom "all families are named."

13. A Summary.

Such, in bare outline, is Southern Buddhism—in its origin a stoical agnosticism which ignored the gods and bade men rely upon themselves in following the paths of goodness that lead to happiness. Because it thus ignored the deepest instincts of humanity, first by turning the thoughts of men away from God, and again by glorifying celibacy, these instincts, refusing to be snubbed, have taken a revenge, so that to-day Buddhism survives, largely because of the teachings it has been compelled to adopt in the process of moulding itself "nearer to the heart's desire." This may be illustrated in two ways. *Nibbāna* at best, originally, an ideal of negative, solitary bliss, has been replaced by an ideal of social life hereafter. Moreover, faith in self-mastery has given place to prayers for help, or, among the most conservative, to the belief that there is a store of merit gained by the sacrificial lives of the Buddhas throughout the ages, which may be "tapped" by the faithful.

Buddhism has thus passed through an interesting history of adjustment. It is important for the student of religion to give close attention to this history, one of the most amazing and fascinating chapters in human thought.

VI. THE MISSIONARY APPROACH TO MODERN BUDDHISM IN SOUTHERN ASIA

I have tried to show both the good and the bad sides of Buddhism in Southern Asia: and have laid emphasis upon those characteristics which demonstrate its continuing power. Southern Buddhists, however, need earnest and sympathetic missionaries, with a gospel of abounding life, of a Father God, and of communion with Him in Christ. Let all who contemplate this great service note the following points.

1. Modern Buddhism differs from the Theoretical Buddhism of Gotama.

There is a marked difference between the theoretical Buddhism of early days, reflected in the standard literature of Southern Buddhism, and the Buddhism of the present day in Southern Asia.

The Buddhism which Western enthusiasts are eager to introduce into their own countries is something which they have learnt, not from the peoples of Buddhist lands, but from the ancient literature of Buddhism. Captivated at first, it may be, by the beauty of some isolated saying, or, possibly, deeply touched during some moonlight scene at the great golden pagodas of Burma or on the hillsides of Ceylon, they become eager and not infrequently learned students of the Buddhism of Gotama. They have to declare with sadness that the great bulk of the people who profess Buddhism have wandered very far from its true principles and practice, and that human nature, for the most part, needs something less austere.

This old Buddhism of the Books may be regarded and used as a kind of Old Testament for Buddhists; already they have passed away from its traditions.

2. The Central Emphasis of Buddhism varies in the Three Southern Countries.

Not only does Buddhism, as the missionary comes in contact with it, differ very markedly from theoretical Buddhism, but the central emphasis varies in different parts of Southern Asia. The student must know his country and his people in order to know their Buddhism, as well as *vice versâ*. Nothing can be further from the sunny temperament of the Burmese than the central "truth" of Buddhism that "all is sorrowful"; and it is a strange perversion of the truth which claims, as some of these Western writers have claimed, that the Burmese are optimistic because they are free from *tanhā*. The fact that they believe in a good Buddha as a living god, however, has much to do with it: and temperament has even more.

In Ceylon, while Buddhist ideals are better suited to the more melancholic temperament of the people, yet they are acutely conscious of their powerlessness to gain the victory over sin and sorrow unaided. As in Japan and China, so in a lesser degree in Burma and Ceylon, Buddhism has been constrained to die to itself (to substitute the idea of a saviour for the idea of earning one's own salvation) in a way that is full of encouragement and suggestion to the Christian. For, if the mythical Kwanyin and the far-off Metteya can so captivate hungry human hearts, how shall not the historic and living Christ be enthroned in their stead?

3. The Qualities of Missionaries to Buddhists.

The life of a missionary to Buddhist peoples is full of interest. Each people has many attractive qualities and the life has much of delight. Certain special qualifications may be worth mentioning :—

(a) *A Genuine Sympathy.*—A missionary will make very little impression upon the people and especially upon their leaders in Buddhist countries who is unable to think himself, to some extent, sympathetically, into their point of view, and to be friendly toward the better aspects of their life and beliefs. There are many things which are "lovely and of good report." The spirit of friendliness and of appreciation goes far toward establishing good relations with the people.

(b) *A Sense of Beauty and of Humour.*—They are

lovers of beauty and enjoy humour, and respond readily to these qualities in the missionary. Moreover, without such gifts life in the tropics is very trying to oneself and to others.

(c) *Christian Convictions.*—Along with these qualities, the missionary must have a passionate loyalty to Christ, a clear understanding of the essential Christian message to such a people, and a firm conviction of the right of Jesus Christ to claim these attractive peoples for God, and to make them great.

(d) *A willingness to appreciate fresh truth.*—It is very desirable that the young missionary should face such people, themselves often creative in their thinking, with a belief that the Holy Spirit, who has guided the nations in their search for truth, is still seeking to lead them on, at least into fresh realisations of the power and meaning of the truths which have meant so much in past ages. Every such missionary will be thrilled in his contact with the inner "soul of the people" to whom he goes, by the hope that they will find in Christ hitherto undiscovered riches and by the desire on his own part to catch something of a continually enlarging vision of Christ and His Church.

4. A Great Opportunity.

The missionary to Buddhists may find encouragement and inspiration in the growing conviction that Oriental Christianity will definitely add strength to the universal Church in coming days. God's kingdom will not be complete without the peoples of Southern Asia. They are deeply religious. It may be far from being an idle dream that God should give to some missionary of to-day the privilege of training a St. Paul, an Origen or an Augustine of the East, who will give to the Church other great chapters of Christian interpretation, and a truly convincing apologetic of the gospel to the world.

II. BUDDHISM IN EASTERN ASIA

I. BUDDHISM IN JAPAN

FROM the Buddhism of Southern Asia to that of China and Japan is a far cry. It must be remembered that the monastic Buddhism, in which the *Arhat* seeking his own salvation is the ideal, gradually gave place before Buddhism left India and entered Eastern Asia to the *Mahāyāna*, or Great Vessel, in which the *Bodhisattva*, or compassionate servant of humanity, became the ideal. Other important changes also took place in the religion of Gotama during the five or six centuries after his death. In the first place, in spite of all his teachings that men should not look to him for help the teacher was himself deified: He "mounts the empty throne of Brahmā." A little later there appeared a docetic tendency which explained him away, or attempted to show that he was without human feeling or passion, a kind of unreal adaptation of the eternal to the needs of time. Others conceived of him as an Eternal Being carrying on the work he had begun upon earth, and opening up salvation to all sentient beings, until finally a trinitarian doctrine was evolved which related the historical Gotama to the eternal Buddha, and conceived of him as having emptied himself of his glory for a season out of compassion for mankind, but as now enjoying it and manifesting it in pitiful and helpful ministries.

It is possible to see in this developing Buddhology evidence of Christian influence: the late Arthur Lloyd of Tokyo is the chief exponent of such a view. To me, however, it seems at once more scientific and more interesting to find in these parallels one more evidence alike of the similarity of human nature in all lands and ages, and of the indwelling Presence of the one Father of us all, guiding the nations in their search for Truth. The vitality and adaptability of Buddhism are evidences of His Spirit.

This vitality, even if at times adaptability has degenerated into compromise, is, as we have seen, great in Southern Asia, and amongst the sources of its strength we have noted its great influence as a civilising power and as a bond of social life: its appeal to the imagination and to the gratitude of the peoples: its philosophical explanation of the age-old problem of suffering, and the moderation and sanity of its ethical teachings. All these factors enter in differing degrees into the vitality of Buddhism in China and Japan: for it has done much to help the civilisation of these countries also, and to give them a popular philosophy of life and a pleasant social setting for religious faith.

Let us consider these facts in more detail as regards the Buddhism of Japan; for she is leading the Orient not only in matters of material progress, but in such spiritual things as a revival of the old faith which she is characteristically using to her own advantage. In 1918, for instance, a Pan-Buddhistic League was formed in Tokyo, and more remarkable has been the lead taken by the Buddhists of Japan in sending strong idealistic appeals to the Conferences at Versailles and Washington. The vital forces of Buddhism in Japan, then, are as follows :—

1. Buddhism has for twelve centuries rendered a unique service to the culture of the nation. Letters, architecture, painting, the discipline of the mind—in fact, the whole culture of Japan is shot through and through with Buddhist influence. It is significant that the two Western writers who entered most deeply into the spirit of Japanese culture, Lafcadio Hearn and Fenollosa, both became Buddhists and are buried in Buddhist cemeteries.

2. Buddhism is again a great bond of social union. Its great pilgrimages, for example, are the favourite recreation of the people, and its great festivals such as the *Bon Matsuri*, in which the spirits of the departed are honoured, are seasons of great sociability. Here, again, the "pessimistic" Buddhism is a cheerful and a pleasant thing.

3. Its appeal to the imagination is obvious. Splendid temples with their dim golden altars, gorgeous vestments, sonorous chanting, and all the splendour of an artistic ritual—all this leaps to the eye of the most casual visitor. What must it not be to the artistic Japanese worshipper with all its tender associations?

4. Nor does Japanese Buddhism appeal less to the mind. Its apologists constantly claim for it that it is a more philosophical and more scientific creed than any other. I have been many times impressed with the wide reading of Japanese Buddhists, and with the intellectual tone of Japanese

Christianity. It is clear that the crude theology of some missionaries will not meet the acid test of modern scholarship, and is partly responsible for a widespread belief amongst the Japanese that Christianity is out of date. The chief Buddhist sects give their priests a better training in the History of Religion than our missionary societies. A stronger apologetic literature is needed.

5. The best apologetic, however, is in saintly lives; Tolstoi and Francis of Assisi especially make an immense appeal to the Japanese; there are Tolstoyan colonies, and a Buddhist Franciscan society. Yet it must be remembered that they find in the saints of Buddhism such as Honen and Nichiren, men worthy to compare with these great Christian souls. Mr. Takayama, whose influence on young Japan has been so great, was at once an ardent disciple of Tolstoy and a follower of Nichiren; Dr. Anesaki is no less a Buddhist of the Nichiren school because he is a devoted admirer of St. Francis. And these men believe that Buddhism and Christianity at their best are closely akin: "We see your Christ," says Dr. Anesaki, "because we have first seen our Buddha."

6. There is much to be said for this view; for Buddhism in Japan has developed a very noble idea of God; he is the Eternal Father who has compassion on all his sons; their salvation is won by faith, not by merit, and gratitude is the motive to good living. It is surely a misnomer to call the fair forms of Amida, the lord of the Western paradise, and of Kwannon the Compassionate, "idols." And Jīzo, the strong Conqueror of Death, the playmate and protector of little children—is he not a

noble embodiment of divine strength and gentleness? If the Christian apologist argues that these are figments of the imagination, the Buddhist is right in replying that they owe their inspiration to the historic Sākyamuni and his early followers, and that there is as much evidence in the vision of a Buddhist saint as in that of an Old Testament prophet for the objective reality of the god who is worshipped. May we not see in the strivings of good and true men everywhere to know God a movement of the Spirit of God Himself? This is my own conviction—that the Spirit of God has been moving for long centuries amongst our Buddhist brethren and has led them far upon the path to Truth. It is, however, only right to say that this view is shared by comparatively few missionaries in Japan. Though the great Conference at Edinburgh in 1910 accepted it as an axiom that God had been at work in these ethnic faiths, and though it was specifically stated of Japanese Buddhism, yet it is a fact that this view is held at best as one of academic interest, and without enthusiasm. The leading authority upon the subject amongst the Protestant missionaries in Japan sums up his conviction in these weighty words and they are one tenable interpretation: "It may be said, then, that Mahāyāna Buddhism is a religion with a rather lofty idea of God among many conceptions of the divine, but without a real faith in the living God; a religion with the idea of a saviour, but without a historical saviour; a religion with a doctrine of divine grace paralysed by the old karma doctrine; a religion with a promise of a present salvation and a future life, which is nevertheless made obscure by the doubts of a recurrent agnostic philosophy that cuts the nerve of all vital ethics and beclouds the hopes of a better future." * The student must weigh these two interpretations: and can only do so by a sympathetic and patient study of the facts. And the outstanding fact is that Buddhism has been the civiliser of Asia, and a great bond of union between its peoples.

Japan is, in many ways, the best country for an intelligent study of its achievements.

She has been called the custodian of Asiatic civilisation: India, China, and Korea have all poured their rich gifts into her lap, and she has preserved them with wise discrimination. But she has always assimilated them till they are her own, and express her own genius. This is perhaps especially true of Buddhism, which is a very different thing in Japan even from what it is in China and Korea. Still more does it differ from that which we have studied in Ceylon and Burma. To turn away from these monastic expressions of the ancient faith to the elaborate Buddhism of Japan is to realise that a development has taken place not unlike that of Christianity, in its transition from the simplicity of Galilean hillsides and the upper chamber at Jerusalem to the pomp of high mass in St. Peter's at Rome or St. Mark's at Venice. Into each great process there have entered similar elements, the growth of a theology by which the historic founder is related to the eternal order, the absorption of ideas and rituals from peoples converted to the new faith and the making over of the faith in each new

* A. K. Reischauer, *Studies in Japanese Buddhism.*

land till it becomes indigenous, and racy of the soil. The story of Buddhism as it developed its philosophical systems and its elaborate pantheon cannot be told here ; * but we may attempt, as in the case of Ceylon and Burma, to give a few impressions of the Buddhism of Japan, which will indicate the processes of change and suggest what are the vital forces of this amazingly flexible religion, whose watchwords have been adaptation and compromise.

When Buddhism entered Japan in the seventh century A.D. it was already the religion of all Asia. It found amidst the semi-barbarous peoples of the islands certain deeply rooted ideas, such as the worship of heroes and especially of the Emperor, who was believed to be descended from the Sun-goddess Amaterasu. Within three centuries it had civilised the country, and had triumphantly identified this goddess with its own Sun-Buddha Vairochana, producing a blended faith made up of elements of the old Shinto (*Shen Tao* or Way of the Gods, *Kami no michi*) and of highly philosophical Buddhism which saw in the sun the source of all cosmic energy. This new Buddhism or *Ryobu Shinto* is different indeed from the faith of the founder, but it claims to be the logical and only legitimate evolution of his teachings.

Let us glance at it first in its great mountain fastness of Kōya San, where its founder Kobo Daishi lived and died, and where the faithful await with him the coming of Miroku—or Maitri—the next Buddha.

* See *Buddhism as a Religion*, by H. Hackmann, and my *Epochs of Buddhist History*. (To be published later.)

Koya San.

Like a great lotus of eight petals are the hills of Kōya San, and up their wooded slopes wind the pilgrim roads. It is the season of pilgrimage and they are thronged with pilgrims clad in white; here is a litter in which some invalid is being borne to the great temple where priests by the performance of mystic ritual and incantations will attempt to restore him to physical as well as spiritual health; here an aged couple are helping one another over steep parts of the way. As they approach the shrines they say a prayer to the pitiful Jizō, that he will be merciful to their dead; then as they pass the wooden octagonal library they turn it upon its axis in order that the merit of reading its voluminous scriptures may be theirs: and near by some afflicted person rubs the portion of the wooden figure of Binzuru which is affected in himself. Behind these somewhat childish superstitions is an elaborate philosophy, and if one is fortunate one may find a monk with leisure and ability to explain the elaborate *mandaras*, the pictures of this *Shingon*, or Trueword; Buddhism. Founded in the ninth century by the great scholar Kobo Daishi, it is a pantheistic worship of Dainichi, the great sun Buddha, the indwelling and pervading essence of the world. Present in all things, he is most present where men worship him, and so by mystic rite and incantation the worshipper is identified with this source of his being, and lays hold of certain secrets of bodily and spiritual health. Japan, like other countries, is eagerly looking for a religion which works, and which has a message for this life as well as for that beyond the grave. Amongst the great trees are innumerable tombs of the faithful, and here in their midst sits Kobo Daishi himself awaiting the coming of Miroku, the next Buddha. Nor is his spirit of loving-kindness, which is the essence of Buddhism, forgotten. Unique amongst the monuments of war stands this seventeenth-century pillar calling down the mercies of heaven upon all who fell in the war with Korea, both friend and foe.

In these temples, too, one will see the simple mirror, emblem at once of Amaterasu and of Dainichi, of Shinto and of Buddhism: are not the two now reconciled, and have they not become an integral part of the soul of Japan, *Yamato Damashii?* Here on Kōyasan mingle Japanese nature-worship, Indian idealistic philosophy, gods from central Asia, and the superstitions of needy human hearts. There is much that is fine as well as much that is corrupt, and it is noteworthy that the impatient reformer, Nichiren, called Kōbo "the prize liar" of Japan, and abominated the beliefs and practices of *Shingon.* Yet he was not unbiased in his judgments!

Hieisan and its Sects.

Another great mountain-fastness of Japanese Buddhism is Hieisan. Here amidst vast cryptomerias and redwoods a contemporary of Kōbo, named Saichō or Dengyō, established just eleven hundred years ago a synthetic Buddhism, which strove to reconcile the conflicting schools and to represent at once the founder Sākyamuni as he is revealed in the Lotus Scripture, seated in glory and opening a way for all to become Buddhas, and the eternal Amida Buddha of the Western Paradise. Side by side are preaching-halls for these two schools of Buddhist devotion, and from the parent stock of *Tendai* have sprung the three great sects of *Jōdo, Shinshu,* and *Nichiren-Shu.* The two former are extreme developments of the Way of Faith in Amida, and the latter is a revolt from their pietism and vain repetitions to the historical Sākyamuni and the famous "Lotus Scripture," the *Hokkekyō* which is found to-day in every Buddhist temple in Japan. At the foot of the great mountain clusters the old imperial city of Kyōto, or Miyako, with its thousand temples. Let us visit some of them.

A Shinshu Temple.

The great *Hondo* or hall of the *Hongwanji* temples in Kyōto is a thing of exquisite beauty. How different are these great altars, these exquisite paintings, this cave of splendour, with its dim lights and its fragrant incense, from the simple rock-hewn shrines of Ceylon and their barbaric frescoes, and from the sunny courtyards and massed images of a Burmese pagoda! Very different, too, is the worship of this devout crowd of Japanese men and women, prostrating themselves before the high altar or joining in antiphonal praises of Amitābha (*Amida Nyorai*), the lord of the Western Paradise. The influence of the solemn chanting, the deep notes of gongs, the incense rising in clouds, the dim lights, the burnished gold and lacquer work of screen and altar—all this is almost hypnotic, and the congregation is borne along on a tide of sombre feeling shot through with gleams of joy and otherworldly enthusiasm. The student who has steeped himself in the simple pithy sayings of the *Dhammapada*, or of the Amitābha Books, and then passes on to study the elaborate apocalypses of the Lotus Scripture, will understand what has taken place in this transition from the simple ethical reform movement of early Buddhism to the elaborate pietism and cultus of the *Mahāyāna*. The historical Sākyamuni has almost disappeared, and in his place there are the eternal or semi-eternal Buddhas, and the great Bodhisattvas. Let us study the figures in this great Kyōto temple. The central position is given to the Japanese monk Shinran, a Luther or Wesley who in the twelfth century popularised in Japan the Way of Salvation by Faith; to the left of him are the figures of Amida Nyorai, the chief object of worship in this sect, Honen, the predecessor of Shinran and his teacher in the way of mystic faith, and Shōtoku, the great layman who as Regent of Japan espoused Buddhism in the seventh century A.D., and laid the foundations of Japanese civilisation. He is the patron saint of the arts and crafts of Japan and is given a prominent place in *Shin Shu* Buddhism (to which three-quarters of Japanese Buddhists belong) because it claims to be a religion for lay-people and not only for monks. There is a delightful story of Shinran and of the lady who led him to realise this truth. Going up to his monastery on the Hiei San Shinran met a charming princess, who took from her long silken sleeve a burning glass; "See how this little crystal gathers to a point the scattered rays of the sun," she cried. "Cannot you do this for our religion?" He replied that it took twenty years to train a monk in the old *Tendai* sect to which he belonged, and she reminded him that women were not allowed to go up to its temples. He went away and meditating upon the essential teachings of Buddhism came to the conclusion that the real heart of the matter was this, that it is faith in the eternal Buddha and gratitude to him which are to be the motives of true living, that as the Lotus Scripture teaches, all may become Buddhas, and that the priests of Amida should be free to become fathers after the pattern of the Heavenly Father. Marrying the charming princess this Japanese Luther founded a new sect, and to-day one sees the hereditary abbot, splendid in purple and scarlet, accompanied by his son, a boy of seventeen, proudly conscious of his destiny as the next head of the great hierarchy, and taking his place in the elaborate ritual of the service. Behind them are the choir in robes of old gold and the priests in black. "*Namu Amida Butsu*" * intone the priests, and alternating with this act of faith they sing to a kind of Gregorian chant such words as these :

> "Eternal Life, Eternal Light !
> Hail to Thee, wisdom infinite.
> Hail to Thee, mercy shining clear,
> And limitless as is the air.
> Thou givest sight unto the blind,
> Thou sheddest mercy on mankind,
> Hail, gladdening Light,
> Hail, generous Might,
> Whose peace is round us like the sea,
> And bathes us in infinity."

* Praise to Amida Buddha.

Or it may be some patriarch who is being hymned, such as Honen himself :

> " What though great teachers lead the way,—
> Genshin and Zendo of Cathay,—
> Did Honen not the truth declare
> How should we far-off sinners fare
> In this degenerate, evil day ? "

Occasionally a hymn, like the excellent preaching of some of the priests, strikes a note of moral living whose motive is gratitude to Amida :

> " Eternal Father on whose breast
> We sinful children find our rest,
> Thy mind in us is perfected
> When on all men thy love we shed ;
> So we in faith repeat thy praise,
> And gratefully live out our days." *

The Japanese, in whom gratitude is a very strong motive, find in the teachings of Shinran a Buddhism which is very Christian, and the words attributed to him as he was nearing his journey's end, are a confession of sin which is only worthy of a saint. That the mass of his followers fall far behind him in this respect is unfortunately true, as it is true of most of us who call ourselves by a greater name.

Other founders of Buddhism are commemorated on the altars and in the hymns of this sect, especially Nāgārjuna, the Indian philosopher of about the second century A.D., and Donran, a Chinese, who carried still further the evolution of Mahāyāna Buddhism.

* See "Buddhist Hymns," tr. by S. Yamabe and L. Adams Beck.

A Revival of Buddhism.

The *Shin Shu* is one of the sects of Japanese Buddhism in which a great revival seems to be at work. Upwards of five hundred young priests are being trained in its schools in Kyōto, and it claims to have one hundred and fifty thousand children in its Sunday Schools, an organisation in which it has wisely imitated the missionary methods of the Christian Church.

This Buddhist revival in Japan is well worthy of study. As in Ceylon and Burma nationalism has much to do with it. The Japanese have been reminded by Lafcadio Hearn and Fenollosa and by their own native scholars trained by Max Müller at Oxford, or in other Western universities, how great is the debt which they owe to Buddhism; "There is scarcely one interesting or beautiful thing produced in the country," wrote Lafcadio Hearn, "for which the nation is not in some sort indebted to Buddhism," and the Japanese, in whom gratitude is a strong motive, are saying, "Thank you." Moreover, in the present restless seeking after truth the nation is finding, in its old religions, things which it is refusing lightly to cast away, and in its resentment against some of the nations of Christendom, and its conviction that our Christianity does not go very deep, it reminds itself that after all Buddhism was a great international force which helped to establish peace for a thousand years in Asia.

The present revival manifests itself in many ways, not least in the new intellectual activity which has brought into existence Buddhist universities, chairs of religious education, and a very vigorous output of literature; and each of the great sects has some outstanding scholar trained in the scientific methods of Western scholarship, but proud to call himself a Buddhist. There are ample signs, too, of a quickened interest in social service, of movements for children and young people, such as the Y.M.B.A., which is now active in all Buddhist countries.

Old temples are being repaired and new ones built and there are said to be over a hundred thousand of these in Japan devoted to Buddhism alone. Amongst the more recent is one in Kyōto which cost nearly a million pounds sterling; for the transport of its massive timbers hundreds of thousands of women sacrificed their hair. It is interesting and amusing to see Buddhist priests in bowler hats and gorgeous robes directing the removal of some ancient shrine to a new site and to note the modern American methods of engineering employed. All this is symptomatic of a new Japan which is yet tenaciously loyal to its old past.

Another symptom is a vigorous attempt at moral reform about which the "Mahāyānist," a Buddhist periodical, said, "Whilst formerly the moral sickness was allowed to go on unchecked, now the coverings are cast aside and the disease laid bare which is the first thing to do if the patient is to be cured." One hears a good deal about misappropriation of temple funds, and moral laxity in matters of sex. It is not for a visitor to comment on these things. Personally I believe that Buddhism is really a power for good: and I am inclined to think that the beautiful courtesy and kindliness one meets everywhere largely spring from it, and are one of its many noble fruits. We in the West have made more of commercial honesty and less of courtesy and forbearance than Jesus was wont to do: and there is no more odious type than the self-righteous visitor from Western lands who comes to the East armed with a narrow and negative moral code and a critical spirit. Certainly Buddhism is teaching "morals" to its children, and in a thousand ways its influence is felt in that very attractive character so truly described by Lafcadio Hearn as peculiar to the Japanese, of which the essence is a genuine kindness of heart that is essentially Buddhist. Another proof that the chief sects are now filled with vigorous life is to be found in their missionary activities. The first Buddhist missionary from Japan to China was sent out by the eastern branch of the *Hongwanji* in 1876, a spiritual return for the early Chinese missions of twelve hundred years ago. Missions have also been established in Honolulu in 1897 and they are numerous on the Pacific Coast of North America. Home missionary work, too, is being attempted, owing largely to the influence of a layman; the *Shin Shu* priests are working in jails, seeking to arouse a sense of sin in the inmates; and in Tokio one may visit a training school where some sixty students are trained in charity organisation and lodging houses for the poor.

Christian Influence.

All this is very largely the outcome of Christian activities in Japan and it is very noteworthy that while the Christian Church is numerically small its leadership in liberal politics and in philanthropy is acknowledged all over the Empire and its pervasive influence upon the thought of modern Japan is obvious on all sides. St. Francis of Assisi and Tolstoy are perhaps the Christian leaders most admired by the Japanese. They belong to the same spiritual company as the great Sākyamuni, who, like them, embraced poverty and was filled with a tender love and a sane yet passionate enthusiasm of humanity. Japan is looking for a great spiritual and moral leader. Will he be a Buddhist like the great Nichiren who in the thirteenth century came like a strong sea-breeze to revive the soul of his people and preached a religion which was to be a moral guide in national affairs and in the daily life of his people? Or will he be a Christian leader who, counting all things as dung compared with the Gospel of Jesus, shall answer the cry of the Japanese patriot who believes that his people are hungry for truth? There is a wealth of liberalism in young Japan and there are idealists everywhere waiting to rally around a great religious leader. But he will need to know and understand her past and to launch his appeal to that wonderful patriotism which is the essence of the Japanese character.

Can Buddhism produce this moral leadership? Let us hear what a Japanese Christian of great learning and insight has to say. "To Buddhism Japan owes a great debt for certain elements of her faith which would scarcely have developed without its aid; but those germinal elements have taken on a form and colouring, a personal vitality not gained elsewhere. Important as are those elements of faith, they still lack the final necessary reality. Buddhism is incomplete in the god whom it presents as an object of worship. In place of the Supreme Being, spiritual and personal, Buddhism offers a reality of which nothing can be affirmed, or, at best, a Great Buddha among many. Buddhism is incomplete in the consciousness of sin which it awakens within the soul of man. Instead of the sense of having violated an eternal law of righteous love by personal antagonism, Buddhism deepens the consciousness of human misery by an unbreakable bond of suffering; and the salvation, therefore, which Buddhism offers is deliverance from misery, not from the power of personal sin. In its idea of self-sacrifice, Buddhism affords an element of faith much more nearly allied to that of the Christian believer. In both the offering of self is for the sake of the multitude, the world-brotherhood; but in the one pity, often acquiescent and helpless, predominates, whereas in the other loyalty to a divine ideal finds expression in the obligation to active service."

And yet let us note that Buddhism has undoubtedly nerved men of action, and inspired saints, and that its call to meditation and to quiet strength is one that our age needs to regard. Not far from the great Pietist temples of *Hongwanji*, I found a veritable haven of peace—the courtyard and simple buildings of a *Zenshu* sect.

How different from the Buddhism of the Amida sects is that of *Zenshu!* Seated in his exquisite retreat one may visit an abbot or teacher of this school. The orderliness and quiet of his temple courts, the stillness of his posture, the repose of his face—all alike tell one of spiritual calm. Perhaps one begins to ask him the secret of it. "Ah," he may say, "that is not easy. You should go and study one of the simpler sects." Then, if his questioner is persistent, he will suddenly present him with one of the *Koans*, or dark sayings which have come down for many centuries: "Listen," he will say, "to the sound of a single hand." Puzzled and disturbed the mind may refuse to deal with this enigma, or it may learn the great lesson which is intended to be learned, that intuition is a surer guide to truth than the discursive reason, or as we should say in our psychological jargon, the sub-conscious has gifts for us if we will give it a chance. The essence, in fact, of this sect is a quiet sense of the presence of eternal truths. The Buddha is not to be found in images or books, but in the heart or mind, and in scores of Buddhist monasteries I have found the spirit of Wordsworth with its serene sense of a pervasive presence,

> "Whose dwelling is the light of setting suns."

II. BUDDHISM IN CHINA

The followers of this meditative school are to be found throughout the monasteries of China and Korea where they are known as the *Chan* sect; but here more than in Japan their quietism is mingled with the devotion to Amitābha or Omito-Fo, and though in many places such as the exquisite island of Putoshan they are faithful in the practice of meditation, they seem to have carried it to a far less perfect pitch than the more scholarly followers of the Japanese school.

A Chinese Temple.

Let us get a glimpse of Chinese Buddhism in one of these great monasteries. The day is a round of worship* and the worship is divided amongst many Buddhas and Bodhisattvas. Here some rich layman is making an offering for masses for his dead; Buddhism in China has indeed become largely a matter of such masses, and the filial Chinese spend yearly scores of millions upon them.† The priests have turned out in force, and the abbot is reciting the praises now of Omito-Fo, now of Pilochana, the great sun-Buddha, now of the merciful Kwanyin whose ears are ever open to human prayer, and now of Titsang, guardian of the dead. Beautiful figures these, and especially that of this strong conqueror of death so popular amongst the Japanese as the guardian of the little ones who have gone into the dark under-world. Innumerable figures of him adorned with baby garments tell their own pathetic tale, and he is unimaginative indeed who cannot find here in these ideal figures traces of the Spirit of God at work in human hearts.

It is harder to sympathise with and to admire the Lama Buddhism which has penetrated China from Tibet, but even here there are some beautiful figures such as the *Tāras*, and amongst the mummery and moral corruption of a Lama temple one may find some sparks of the divine spirit, even if one fails to meet the Lama of Kim!

Buddhism in China, decadent though it is in

* The chief services are at 2 a.m. and at 4 p.m.

† During the war many such masses were said for the fallen, whether friend or foe.

many places, is reviving itself; there is great building activity at certain centres such as Ningpo and Hangchow; there are probably nearly half a million monks, and at one ordination in 1920 a thousand candidates were ordained in Changchow. Many men, indeed, disillusioned at the failure of the revolution, are seeking the quiet otherworldly retreats of Buddhism, and others of scholarly bent delight in the classical scriptures which the early missionaries from India translated into Chinese, and which are still models of beauty.

Among laymen also there is an increasing interest in the Buddhist scriptures. Turn into this book-store at Peking and you will find over a thousand copies of different texts and commentaries, and there are publishing-houses in most of the great cities. Two notable works are the reprint of the whole of the Scriptures and a new dictionary of Buddhist terms, containing over three thousand pages. At Ningpo one will find a small group of young enthusiasts working for a "neo-Buddhism." Antipathetic to Christianity, and especially to the aggressions of "Christian" nations, these men, like some of the propagandists in Ceylon, use weapons which are two-edged and dangerous to all religion, not only to Christianity; they seem to feed upon the publications of the rationalist press, and must not be taken too seriously. Yet we can sympathise with their resentment of Western aggression, which is a large factor in these Buddhist movements everywhere. "Buddhism: the Religion of Asia" often accompanies and reinforces another cry, "Asia for the Asiatics."

Of great significance are these Pan-Buddhist

movements attempting to unite the Buddhist peoples in a strong Eastern civilisation such as that which welded them together for a thousand years in the Golden Age of the past. One such movement originates in Ceylon with the vigorous layman Dharmapala, in whom resentment against the West blends with a real enthusiasm for Buddhism. In 1893 he visited China, and stirred up some of the Chinese monks, calling upon them to go to India as missionaries; in Japan he attacked some of the great abbots as wine-drinkers and corrupt, and everywhere he is a pungent and provocative influence. In 1918 a Pan-Buddhist Association was started in Tokyo and in the following year a rival one was founded in Peking. It is, in fact, rather pathetic to find Buddhism being promoted by the Japanese in Korea as a part of their propaganda to Japanise the Koreans, and at the same time claiming in China to be *the* religion for democratic nations.

In justification of such claims, however, Buddhism is doing some good work in social service, and in education, and takes its part in famine relief, prison visitation, and the beneficent work of the Red Cross.

The Chinese are a religious people, whatever critics may say. Vast armies of monks and innumerable temples and shrines witness to this other-worldly strain, and though much of their religion is superstitious, and almost all of it needs moralising, the sympathetic observer will find on every hand the evidences that these are not a "secular-minded" people.

In almost every house are not only ancestor-tablets, but images of Kwanyin and other Buddhist deities, and pilgrimages play in China as elsewhere in Asia a great part in the national life.

Follow this merry throng as it climbs the slopes of some great mountain; note the groves and the poetical inscriptions on the rocks; enter this noble group of temples with them and watch their acts of worship.

Here before Kwanyin a young apprentice bows: carelessly he tosses the bamboo strips which will tell him if his prayer is to be answered, and defiantly he tosses his head as he turns away with a refusal from the goddess: but here is an old widow, with sorrowful persistence importuning the Compassionate One, and in even the most careless is a belief that Heaven rules in the affairs of men and that Heaven is just.

Here prayers are offered for rain and harvest, for children and wealth, for release from suffering and demons.

As in many Christian nations the bridge between natural religion and the essential truths of Christian Theism is a very shaky one—so here in China and Japan, whilst there is a widespread belief in Karma and in Heaven's laws, this is but vaguely connected with the polytheistic cults of the masses. And as in some other Christian lands, the worship of the saints and local gods—even of the great Kwanyin—is not always moralised. Habitual sinners—opium fiends who, it may be, are ruining scores of lives, prostitutes and murderers—will pay their daily court to the family or local god: not conscious of any demand from the Compassionate that they should show compassion, or from the Righteous that they should be righteous. Buddhism has indeed lost its early salt of morality. It is for these and other reasons that China and Japan urgently need the Gospel of Jesus and of His Kingdom. In their own religious development is a noble preparation for this New Order: and in the Jesus of History they are finding a Norm and a Vision of God which makes their old ideals real and vital, and which purifies their idea of God. In this faith the Church is at work in these wonderful lands, believing that they have rich gifts for the Kingdom of God, and that it will greatly enrich them and carry to its fulfilment their noble civilisations whilst it emancipates their masses from fear and superstition. With all its achievements Buddhism has failed because it has had no power to cast out fear, and its Confucian critics even accuse it of playing upon the superstition of the people and of letting loose more demons to plague them. Yet it has done much for China, not only ennobling her art and culture but giving a new value to the individual, a new respect for women, a new love of nature, and many noble objects of worship to hungry human hearts.

Whilst then the Gospel wins its way slowly but surely in Asia, leavening and giving new and abundant life, there are those in Christendom who hold that it is played out, and that Buddhism is destined to supersede it as the religion of the intelligent!

The student should investigate their activities in London, Breslau, and other Western cities; and he may find Appendix I a finger-post to guide him in his quest.

Appendix II is offered as a similar guide to a course of reading.

APPENDIX I *

SOME EUROPEAN AND AMERICAN BUDDHISTS

IN the year 1881 Dr. Rhys Davids said, "There is not the slightest danger of any European ever entering the Buddhist Order." † Yet a recent writer was told by a Buddhist in Ceylon that his religion was making its converts "chiefly amongst the Tamils and Germans," and in each of the Buddhist countries there is to-day a small but active group of converts from the European nations to Buddhism.

It would be difficult to say whether these groups are the product or the cause of the undoubted revival which is taking place in the Buddhist world: probably they are part product and part cause. Buddhism is certainly in ferment. As Dr. Suzuki has said, "It is in a stage of transition from a mediæval dogmatic and conservative spirit to one of progress, enlightenment, and liberalism," ‡ and in other ways, especially in Japan, it is approximating to a liberal Christianity.

To this awakening there are several contributory causes, such as the national spirit which has awakened in recent years, the works of Eastern and Western students of Buddhism, the activities of the Theosophical Society, and, it must be confessed, and unwise and, in my opinion, illiberal and unfair attitude on the part of many missionaries who, forgetting that they are sent to preach Christ, have attacked, often without adequate knowledge, the

* Reprinted from *The East and the West.*

† *Hibbert Lectures*, 3rd edition, p. 184.

‡ *The Zen Sect of Buddhism*, p. 11.

religion of Gautama.* From this criticism I do not wish to exempt myself; I have gone through the unpleasant but salutary process of having to eat my own words, and I am more anxious than I can say to foster a real spirit of love and understanding between the followers of Gautama and those of Jesus.

Of the founder of Buddhism I can honestly say with the great Danish scholar Fausböll: "The more I know of him, the more I love him," and it is the "fact of Gautama," emerging more and more clearly as the Buddhist books are being edited and translated, which more than any other single cause is responsible for the Buddhist revival.

"From such far distances the echo of his words returns that we cannot but rank him amongst the greatest heroes of history," says the eminent Belgian scholar de la Vallée Poussin, and from him, as from Gautama, we shall all do well to learn the spirit of tolerance and courtesy. Yet both of them speak out bluntly and shrewdly enough at times. It is recorded that when the great teacher met men whose doctrines were morally dangerous or intellectually insincere, he harried them remorselessly till "the sweat poured from them" and they cried, "As well might one meet an infuriated bull or dangerous snake as the ascetic Gautama!" Of those whose teachings were sincere and earnest he was wonderfully tolerant, even advising a soldier disciple to give alms to them and their followers, no less than to the Buddhist monks.

In this spirit the Belgian scholar, probably the greatest living authority upon Buddhism as a whole, is lovingly tolerant towards Buddhism and honest

* There is fortunately a marked improvement in this respect in missionary methods: but the old order has not yet given place to the new. The present writer was recently classed, in a public address in Rangoon, with the Kaiser and Antichrist—as a "Sign of the Times."

Buddhists, but of Neo-Buddhism he says: "It is at once frivolous and detestable—dangerous, perhaps, for very feeble intellects." Even so, a vast Neo-Buddhist Church is not impossible!

European and American Buddhists, then, fall into these two classes: those who are honest and sincere students of Buddhism and followers of Gautama, and those of whom the most charitable thing that can be said is that they lead astray "foolish women," and other sentimentalists. To illustrate the methods of these two schools, who are unfortunately at present often working in an unnatural alliance, let me describe two recent experiences.

On Easter Day I went from the simple and exquisite beauty of our Communion Service, in which the glamour of the Resurrection is ever being renewed, to a Buddhist church within a stone's throw, here in the heart of San Francisco. There, as in innumerable other centres of Buddhist life, the birth of Gautama was being celebrated; and I could unhesitatingly join in paying reverence to the memory of the great Indian teacher. But it was certainly amazing and a little staggering to find "Buddhist High Mass" being performed, the celebrant calling himself a bishop and ordaining on his own initiative abbots and abbesses.* Three altar candles representing the Buddha, the Law, and the Order being lighted, the "bishop," preceded by seven or eight American and British monks in yellow robes, and by the Abbess, known as Mahadevi, ascended to the platform, which contains a beautiful Japanese shrine of the Hongwanji sect. Several monks from Japan, to my surprise, assisted in the strange service that followed, which began with the invocation of Amida Buddha, and went on in an astonishing hotch-potch of the cults of

* The full form of service and a biographical sketch of its author is published by the *Open Court*, Chicago, U.S.A.

the primitive and the later Buddhism derived indiscriminately from Ceylon, Tibet, and Japan.

Of this strange service, which the "bishop" claims to have modelled on that in use in the Dalai Lama's palace at Lhassa, it must suffice to say that if the Tibetan *Mantras* were as inaccurately rendered as were the five precepts in Pāli which are the Buddhist pentalogue, then the general impression of Buddhism given was as misleading as it is possible to conceive. The service included a processional hymn, music by an organist announced as "late of the Golden Temple Shway Dagon in Burma, and of St. Paul's Cathedral, London," an "Epistle" read by an American Buddhist, a "gospel of the day," read by the Abbess, several addresses by Japanese and Western Buddhists, and a sermon by the "bishop," who claims to be ninety-five years old, to be the son of a Persian prince, to have spent sixteen years at the feet of the late Dalai Lama in Tibet, to have numerous degrees in arts, medicine, science, and philosophy from Oxford, London, Paris, and Heidelberg, and to have been seventy-five years a monk of the yellow robe. His costume was as amazingly mixed as his liturgy, consisting of a Hindu turban, a yellow Buddhist overmantle, a scarlet robe with cincture and maniple of purple, and a rosary terminating in the *Swastika*, with which sign he blessed the people at the end of the service, saying: "May the face of the Truth shine upon you, and the divine Wisdom of the Buddhas permeate you, and remain with you now and throughout eternity. So mote it be."

In his sermon he claimed to have founded no less than eighty missions in the past ten years in California, and said some shrewd things in criticism of the Christian Church, of which I am persuaded he was himself once a member. For the rest it was a practical discourse enough; he advised his followers, if they would live as long as he (and he announced that he would still be going strong fifty years hence), they must change their wrinkles into dimples, and learn the secret of a serene mind. He gave notice that in the evening there would be a banquet and a dance, in which he would join, if widows and maidens pressed him, and immediately after the service he saluted them all " with a holy kiss," which they seemed to enjoy as much as he. There is something really attractive about this jovial monk, and he has the energy, the ubiquity and the perseverance of another " Persian prince " who is equally opposed to Christianity!

The " bishop's " disciples are fairly numerous, though one of his colleagues expressed the conviction, on the authority of an English professor, that the same wonderful teachings would draw thousands to hear them in London, instead of scores in San Francisco. Be that as it may, they are faithful disciples; attracted very largely by the fact that he is rather expounding spiritualism, telling of the wonderful *Mahatmas* of Tibet, and luring them with the glamour of Eastern mysticism than teaching Buddhism. When I chuckled at some of his shrewd sallies, an elegantly dressed woman next to me said, " Hush! Hush! You are not an initiate, you do not understand; all that he says has a profound, inner meaning which only we who are initiated can comprehend." To which I could not resist the reply: " I may not be initiated into this business, but I know that this is not Buddhism any more than that the organist who is playing those penny-whistle tunes on the harmonium ever played them on the Shway Dagon, where music is not allowed, or any more than the old sportsman who is speaking is a bishop."

It is not by such means that Buddhism can be revived.

But there are others! Some years ago I had a delightful talk with one of them in the shadow of the great pagoda from which our organist did not come. He was a Scot, a scholar and scrupulously honest, and his name is already widely known as the translator of both German and Pāli works. Quite frankly he told me why he had taken the yellow robe, and how, having lost his faith in Christianity, he found in the Buddhist books something which saved his reason and probably his life: then, turning to me, he said: "How glad you fellows would be if you could get rid of the Old Testament."

Another friend of mine, an Englishman, was formerly trained as a Roman Catholic priest, and is now a Buddhist missionary in California, having been ordained in Japan, and having, with an American scholar, now a professor in London, been responsible for the production of an admirable and scholarly periodical, *The Mahayanist.* Its object is to impart an accurate knowledge of the Buddhism of China and Japan, and to investigate its history, doctrines, and present conditions in an unbiased and scholarly way.

Such men as these three ought not to be associated with those who claim to teach "esoteric" Buddhism.* There is really no such thing; "I have preached the Law without making any distinction between exoteric and esoteric doctrine," said Gautama, "for I have no such thing as the closed fist of the teacher who keeps some things in reserve." †

Now so long as these unequally yoked teams are drawing the Buddhist chariot, there is bound to be a smash; when one studies, for instance, the history of the propagandist literature they have put out, one finds that it is one long story of fitful beginnings and spasmodic effort, almost all of them failing to survive for more than a few years. Of these periodicals, Professor Poussin writes as follows: "Propagandist reviews

* They are, fortunately, even now parting company: the "bishop," for example, has been obliged to start a rival "church" in San Francisco.

† From the *Mahaparinibbana Sutta*, the oldest and most authentic of the Buddhist scriptures.

like *Buddhism* of Rangoon and the *Open Court* of Chicago are useful when Mrs. Rhys Davids condescends to contribute to them, but she finds in them strange neighbours indeed, fully worthy of the indescribable Mahabodhi Society ! "

Buddhists everywhere are finding new inspiration by going back to the authority of Gautama ; let the Christian Church go back to Jesus Christ, and, taking Him as the full and perfect revelation of the nature of God and man, rethink and restate its theology. And secondly, let its missionaries study the great religion of Gautama—which is still, after twenty-five centuries, a mighty power, with strong capacity for revival, and which is still strangely misunderstood ; and let them see to it that they and the Christian " native " pastors and catechists are as carefully trained as the Buddhist monks who each year are receiving a more systematic preparation for the task of defending and propagating the *Dhamma*.

APPENDIX II

HOW TO STUDY BUDDHISM *

THE Christian missionary in Buddhist lands is faced with a task of infinite fascination. He is dealing, in the first place, with remarkable peoples for whom their religion has done much of the great service which Christianity has done for him and his people. He will find everywhere traces of a mighty Buddhist civilisation, and in many places, if he has the eye to see, proofs that this venerable religion is still alive and is reforming itself to meet the needs of the modern world. In the second place, he will find that it is vitally linked up with the intensely interesting and important nationalist movements of Asia, and that he cannot understand the political situation in these countries without a close and careful study of the religion. And in the third place, he will find that it is not only as part and parcel of nationalist movements that Buddhism is alive, but that it has an international programme and that it is closely bound up with the movement of " Asia for the Asiatics " —a movement deserving of respectful and sympathetic study.

How then will the missionary prepare himself for this absorbing task? Nothing can take the place of friendly intercourse with Buddhists in temple and home,

* Reprinted by kind permission of the editors and publisher from "An Introduction to Missionary Service," Ed. by G. A. Gollock and E. G. K. Hewat, Oxford University Press. 1921, 3*s*. 6*d*. net.

on pilgrimage and at great times of festival; it is thus that the religion will become a living reality to him, full of colour and movement, giving him at times moments of exquisite pleasure in its artistic pageantry, and bringing him into sympathetic touch with the "soul of the people" to whom he is seeking to minister. But to prepare him for this absorbing pursuit, at once business and pleasure, study and hobby, for any one who really enjoys such things, he can and must do some systematic reading. Appended are a course of study for the first two years worked out for Y.M.C.A. secretaries in India, and a more advanced and detailed course. The following additional notes may be of service in using these:

1. Clearly the first step is to get a sympathetic and accurate idea of the founder of Buddhism, of the essence of his teaching, and of the secret of his amazing influence. There is, in human history, only one figure more significant and more worthy of a study. Side by side the student should read Sir Edwin Arnold's *Light of Asia* (London: Kegan Paul. 1*s*. 6*d*. and 5*s*.) and some good biographical study such as that of H. Oldenberg, *Buddha* (London: Williams & Norgate. Out of print. 1882), or that by the present writer, *Gotama Buddha* (New York: Association Press. 1920).

2. Next he will do well to saturate himself in such selections of the moral teachings of Gautama as are contained in the *Dhammapada* or the *Itivuttaka*, both of which contain much very early material, some of which may be attributed to the founder himself.

3. For the whole Buddhist system in its earlier forms Warren's admirable *Buddhism in Translations* (Harvard Oriental Series. Cambridge, Mass., U.S.A. 1900) is indispensable, and should be constantly used for reference.

4. As an introduction to the history of Buddhism two elementary books, attempting to cover the whole field in a rather sketchy way, are Saunders' *The Story of Buddhism* (London: Oxford University Press.

4*s*. 6*d*. 1916) and Hackmann's *Buddhism as a Religion* (London: Probsthain. 15*s*. 1910).

5. Whether the student is going to work in lands devoted to the primitive type of Buddhism, such as Ceylon, Siam, and Burma, or in those in which a highly developed Buddhism prevails, such as Japan, China, and Korea, he ought to have a grasp of the essential differences between the two types of Buddhism known as *Hinayāna* and *Mahāyāna;* for an evolution must be read backwards as well as forwards, and the missionary will look forward to spending a holiday in one of the other Buddhist lands. If, for instance, his lot is cast in Burma, he ought to plan to go on a visit to Japan or to China, and *vice versâ.* To get a grasp of the highly developed Mahāyāna he should study especially the famous *Lotus of the Good Law* translated in vol. xxi of the Sacred Books of the East (Oxford: Clarendon Press. 15*s*. 6*d*.) and should carefully compare this with the *Dhammapada*. He will find that even in the conservative Buddhism of Ceylon and Burma there are Mahāyāna tendencies, and that everywhere Gautama Buddha has become in practice more than a moral teacher and is related, in the minds of the people, to an eternal order making for righteousness. In this and in other ways which the student will study for himself, *e.g.* in the idea of a sacrificial life-process culminating in the historical life of Sākyamuni and in the practice of prayer by all Buddhists, he will find a wonderful preparation for the gospel of Christ. I would suggest that he take as his guiding light this saying of a great Buddhist scholar of Japan, "We see your Christ, because we have first seen our Buddha." The task of the missionary will be to relate Christianity to this great preparation that has been made for it and to think out with Eastern scholars the thought bases of a truly Eastern Christianity which shall seem to these Asiatic nations to come with all the authority of their own past behind it, and with all the glamour of a knowledge that

the God who has been working with and for them in the past is now bringing them out into a larger and freer life. Only so can they be won for Christ.

I

The following course of reading—drawn up for Secretaries of the Y.M.C.A. in the East by Dr. J. N. Farquhar and the writer—is recommended to those whose leisure is scant :

First Year. General : Rhys Davids, *Buddhism, Life and Teachings of Gautama, the Buddha* (London : S.P.C.K. 3*s.* 6*d.*) ; V. Smith, *Asoka* (Oxford : Clarendon Press. 4*s.* New edition, 1920).

Special : *The Dhammapada.* Sacred Books of the East, vol. x (out of print) ; *The Mahaparinibbana.* S.B.E., vol. xi (12*s.* 6*d.* See Introduction).

Additional : Oldenberg, *Buddha* (see Introduction) ; or Rhys Davids, *Dialogues of the Buddha* (London : Milford. 12*s.* 6*d.* 3rd volume, 1921).

Second Year. General : Copleston, *Buddhism Primitive and Present* (London : Longmans. 10*s.* 6*d.* Out of print) ; Hackmann, *Buddhism as a Religion* (see Introduction).

Special : Warren, *Buddhism in Translations.* Chaps. i and iv (see Introduction).

Additional : Rhys Davids, *Buddhist India* (London : Fisher Unwin. 7*s.* 6*d.*) ; *The Questions of King Milinda,* S.B.E., vols. xxxv, xxxvi. (42*s.* for two. See Introduction.)

II

For those who desire further and more detailed study the following suggestions, based upon Professor Hume's course at Union Theological Seminary and the present writer's at the Pacific School of Religion, are likely to prove helpful :

A. *The Life of the Buddha.*

Rhys Davids, *Buddhism, Life and Teachings of Gautama, the Buddha*, chaps. ii, iii, vii (see I, *First Year*); Kern, *Manual of Indian Buddhism*, part ii (London: Probsthain. 15*s.*); Oldenberg, *Buddha*, part i (see Introduction); Warren, *Buddhism in Translations*, chap. i (see Introduction); Saunders, *Gotama Buddha* (see Introduction).

B. *The Scriptures of Hinayāna Buddhism.*

The Vinaya Pitaka (Discipline Basket), The Sutta Pitaka (Teaching Basket), The Abhidhamma Pitaka (Higher Religion, or Metaphysical Basket).

Rhys Davids, *Buddhism, Its History and Literature* (London: Putnams. 10*s.* 6*d.* 1907); Hastings' *Encyclopædia of Religion and Ethics*, vol. viii, pp. 85–9 (Edinburgh: T. and T. Clark. 35*s.* 1916); K. J. Saunders, *Heart of Buddhism* (London: Oxford University Press. 2*s.* 6*d.* Calcutta: Association Press. 6*d.* 1915); Sacred Books of the East, vols. x, xi, xvii, xix, xx, xxi, xxxv, xxxvi, xlix (see Introduction); Rhys Davids, *Sacred Books of the Buddhists*, vols. ii, iii (London: Milford. 12*s.* 6*d.* each).

C. *The Doctrines and Practices of Hinayāna Buddhism.*

(The Hindu Setting, Moral Teachings, Concerning the Soul, Transmigration, Karma, Nirvana, Methods of Salvation, Prayer, Miracles, The Order Woman.)

Rhys Davids, *Buddhism, A Sketch*, chaps. iv, v, vi (London: Williams and Norgate. 2*s.* 6*d.* 1912); E. W. Hopkins, *Religions of India*, chap. xiii (Boston: Ginn & Co. 10*s.* 6*d.* 1902); K. J. Saunders, *Buddhist Ideals* (Calcutta: Y.M.C.A., 10 annas. 1912).

D. *The Expansion of Buddhism.*

(In India, the Adjacent Countries, in China and Korea, in Japan.)

K. J. Saunders, *Story of Buddhism*, chaps. iv, vii (see Introduction); Hackmann, *Buddhism as a Religion*, Book iii (see Introduction); Rhys Davids, *Buddhism, Sketch*, chap. ix (see C); R. F. Johnston, *Buddhist China* (London: Murray. 18*s*. 1913); K. Reischauer, *Japanese Buddhism* (London and New York; Macmillan. 10*s*. 6*d*. $2. 1917).

E. *Differences between Hinayāna and Mahāyāna.*

Suzuki, *Outlines of Mahāyāna* (London: Lusac. 8*s*. 6*d*. Out of print. 1908); *Encyclopædia of Religion and Ethics*. Under headings (see B).

F. *Buddhism and Christianity.*

(Similarities and Differences.)

Saunders, *Buddhist Ideals* (see C); Carus, *Buddhism and its Christian Critics*, chap. v (Chicago: *Open Court* Publishing Co. 7*s*. 6*d*.); K. J. Saunders, *Story of Buddhism*, chap. viii (see Introduction).

III

For still more detailed work see the excellent booklets prepared by the Board of Missionary Preparation, 25 Madison Avenue, New York City, *The Preparation of Missionaries to Buddhist Lands* and *Buddhism and Buddhists in China*—both in the press.